GOODBYE stress HELLO LIFE!

Allan Kehler
B.Ed., B.PhEd.

Printed in Canada
5 6 7 8   22 23 24 25

Library and Archives Canada Cataloguing in Publication

Kehler, Allan, 1981-, author
    Goodbye stress, hello life! / Allan Kehler.

Includes bibliographical references. ISBN 978-1-927756-53-9 (paperback)

    1. Stress (Psychology). 2. Stress (Psychology)—Prevention.
I. Title.

BF575.S75K43 2016   155.9'042   C2016-900855-X

Editing, layout and design by Heather Nickel
Front cover image © shutterstock.com/ 65905426/Dudarev Mikhail

Interior images:
Chapter 1: sympathetic vs parasympathetic © Allan Kehler
Chapter 2: stuck on and off © Allan Kehler
Chapter 3: signs of stress © Allan Kehler
Chapter 4: stress vs performance © Allan Kehler
Chapter 5: © shutterstock.com/ 252246103/PathDoc
Chapter 6: who am I wheel © Allan Kehler
Chapter 7: path to healing © Allan Kehler

www.allankehler.com

YOUR NICKEL'S WORTH PUBLISHING

Regina, SK.

www.ynwp.ca

MIX
Paper from
responsible sources
FSC® C103214

For Tanya—my wife and best friend.
Thank you for always believing in me,
and for showing me what it really means to live.

Author's Note

It is inevitable that we will experience stress in life. The difference is that some people sit in the middle of their stress with little motivation to change, and others search for tools to assist in their ability to change. My hope is that this book can provide you with a set of tools that will allow you to enjoy your journey.

I encourage you to reflect on your own experiences, and think about what you want in life. You are the only one who has the power to create your own reality. It is my hope that chapters 1 and 2 will help you to understand the way stress works, while the remaining chapters will provide you with tools to manage your stressors, guide you through change, and empower you to live opposed to merely exist.

While I do provide some basic information on stress, the thoughts expressed in this book are based on my own personal and professional experiences. Names and stories have been changed to protect the confidentiality of those involved.

Contents

Introduction

Imagine that you frequently experience stomach pain. If you repeatedly reach for an aspirin in an attempt to alleviate your pain, you are only masking the root cause. Would it not be more effective to take a step back and think about what is causing the stomach pain in the first place? The solution might require nothing more than a change in diet. In the same way, you may experience stress but struggle to identify, or hesitate to change, what is causing your stress in the first place.

I frequently meet people who dread going to their workplace, and yet they continue entering the same doors. Others are unhappy with their relationships, and yet they remain. Why would someone stay in a position or situation that causes them immense stress and fails to bring them happiness?

When I ask my clients this question, I hear two common responses. One, they have become complacent and believe they will never find anything better. Two, they believe they are not worthy of anything better, or do not deserve a life of happiness.

For years, I struggled to believe that I was worthy of a life of happiness, and failed to accept that life was something that could be enjoyed. Thankfully, I have finally come to understand that I *am* worthy, and have arrived at a point where I can say it is good to be alive.

The key was that I had to create this reality.

Take a moment to sit back and reflect on your surroundings. From your material possessions to your relationships, you have created it all. You are the creator of your own reality and your own happiness. If you are not content with your life, you are the only one who is in a position of power to create a different outcome.

What do you want in life? It is yours to create.

This is *your* journey.

"It's not the load that breaks you down. It's the way you carry it."

— Lou Holtz

1

UNDERSTANDING STRESS

The Stress Response

Stress is a normal part of life. In fact, your very birth into this world likely occurred in a complete state of stress! Stress is simply the body's response to any physical or emotional demand, whether real or imagined.

Although stress is usually perceived in a negative light, there are actually some positives that can come from it. In the right dosage, stress can be just what the body needs to get blood flowing and to create the feeling of being alive.

When your body's stress response is working properly, it helps you to stay focused, alert, and energetic. It allows you to stay motivated and meet whatever challenges the day may bring.

In moments of crisis or unexpected threats, it is your body's response to stress that can actually save your life. For example, there are stories of people who have found the superman-like strength needed to lift a car in an effort to save another person.

Thankfully, your body is designed to experience stress and react to it accordingly. When you sense danger, your body automatically activates a process known as the "fight-or-flight" reaction, also known as the stress response. This is a survival mechanism and helps prepare us for life-threatening situations. The human body views stress as a threat to its survival, and the brain responds by releasing a flood of stress hormones, including cortisol and adrenaline, to prepare the body for a potential emergency.

Unfortunately, the body can also overreact and activate this same response to non-life-threatening events such as trying to meet deadlines at work or preparing for that big exam.

The Systems at Work

The body's autonomic nervous system controls involuntary functions such as breathing, blood pressure, and heartbeat. This system has two components: sympathetic and parasympathetic.

The sympathetic system acts like a gas pedal. During a stressful event, it is activated to increase an individual's chance of survival. One instinct may be to run (i.e. flight). Another may be to face the stressor directly (i.e. fight). The third instinct is to do nothing (i.e. freeze).

In contrast, the parasympathetic system acts like a brake. When it is activated, the body enters a state of gradual relaxation. This is what allows the body to calm down once it is convinced that the threat has passed.

The image below demonstrates a healthy nervous system and is based on the work of Dr. Peter Levine, author of *Waking the Tiger: Healing Trauma.*

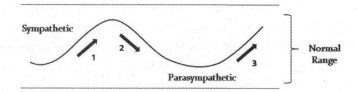

Consider the example of driving your car only to be suddenly cut off by another vehicle. The first arrow indicates that the sympathetic system has become activated in the face of a potential threat. This threat will immediately cause your blood pressure and heart rate to increase, and may also sharpen your focus. If you have had a similar experience, think about how your body reacted.

Let's say that you manage to avoid the collision after a close call, and your body recognizes that the threat is over. The second arrow indicates the parasympathetic system kicking in, bringing your body back to a state of balance. The third arrow demonstrates how the cycle is again repeated with each new threat, once again activating the sympathetic system.

This is how a healthy nervous system functions. When your system is in balance, you have choices and options. After the sympathetic system is activated, the body has the tools to self-regulate, which allow the parasympathetic system to kick in to return you to your initial state of balance.

Unfortunately, the systems of individuals who have experienced significant trauma do not regulate in this manner. Trauma may come in many forms, such as involvement in war, a car accident, a major surgery, or an abusive or violent home environment. These traumatic life events can prevent an individual from coping effectively with other stressful life circumstances.

Think about a child raised in a violent home environment. Children are not in a position of power or control, and are at the mercy of the adults in the home. If a young girl is confronted and abused by someone bigger and stronger, the options of fight or flight are not available to her. Her only remaining option is to freeze.

Sadly, no nurturing adult is there to teach this young child how to calm down. No one is there to comfort her and make her feel safe enough to allow the negative feelings stored after the trauma to be released.

Uncertain whether this event will happen again, her body remains on high alert. Her parasympathetic system does not have a chance to kick in, and she can become "stuck on," as though her foot constantly pushes down on a gas pedal. When this occurs, she may experience anxiety, an inability to relax, difficulty sleeping, or trouble focusing.

For some individuals, it is also possible for the other extreme to occur, and the parasympathetic system takes over. This causes the individual to become "stuck off." In this case, they experience minimal emotional response, lethargy, chronic fatigue, or depression.

The graphic below is modified from the works of Dr. Peter Levine and indicates how an unhealthy nervous system responds to stress:

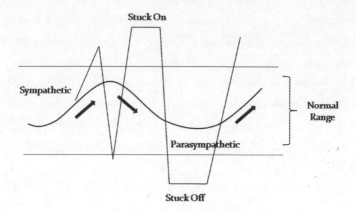

If the system is unable to provide the individual with a sense of balance, the person has to find their own ways to self-regulate. If their system is "stuck on," they need to find something to bring them back down. Alcohol, which is a central nervous system depressant, can serve as a quick fix. Others find themselves impulsively engaging in self-harming behaviours, such as cutting, as a coping mechanism to provide an emotional release.

On the other hand, if the system is "stuck off," substances like cocaine or amphetamines, which are central nervous system stimulants, can bring them back up. Individuals may also engage in other activities that provide an immediate rush or sense of pleasure through activities such as gambling, sex, or excessive food consumption. Over time, this internal need to self-regulate has the potential to lead to an addiction.

Signs of Stress

Life can be very demanding, and in this fast-paced world sometimes it is hard to stop and take time to listen to what your mind and body are telling you. It can often be easier for you to identify stress in others than in yourself. Stress symptoms may also be difficult to recognize because they have now become "normal" for you. As a result, you may not even be aware that you are under any stress in the first place. The following chart reflects some signs of stress in three key areas:

Physical	Psychological	Behavioural
Headaches	Irritable	Isolation
Clenched jaw	Anxiety	Over- or under-eating
Muscle tightness	Mood swings	Impatience
Shortness of breath	Decreased motivation	Fidgeting
Fatigue or insomnia	Distracted	Substance abuse

Effects of Stress

Stress is subjective in nature. What one individual might perceive as a small stressor may be perceived by another as insurmountable.

Have you ever found that it is difficult to think clearly when you are under a significant amount of stress? Psychologically, many individuals under high levels of stress find themselves struggling to concentrate and accomplish tasks that used to be done with ease. Too much stress affects the normal functioning of your prefrontal cortex, the part of your brain where thoughts are processed and behaviours are regulated. This is why it may become difficult to process information and maintain normal functioning. This can also cause you to make decisions that you might later regret.

A friend of mine, Jason, was the principal of an elementary school in a small town. The school year was nearing its end and he was feeling overloaded with responsibilities. One day, a Grade 2 student decided to test his authority. While students were filing onto the buses in front of the school, this seven-year old stood defiantly in front of Jason with a soccer ball in his hands. Both Jason and the boy were well aware of the rule that all balls were to remain in the school following the last bell of the day.

This daring young boy tauntingly tossed the soccer ball up and down in front of Jason's face. Using a stern voice, Jason asked the boy to return the ball to the school. The boy shook his head "no" with a devious grin. Jason lowered his chin, pointed toward the school doors, and loudly demanded that he take the ball back into the school immediately.

By this time, some students had begun to take note of the altercation. Feeding off this attention, the boy smiled, spun around, and proceeded to kick the soccer ball into the air in the direction of the school. The ball landed on the roof, their eyes met, and the young boy took off running as though his life depended on it. In a state of absolute fury, Jason chased after him.

The boy hopped onto his bike and began rapidly peddling past the school buses full of curious eyes observing the drama unfold in front of them. Without thinking, Jason selected the closest kid's bike, and peddled furiously after the boy, knees ramming against the handlebars. The students watched in anticipation from the sidewalks and bus windows as their principal chased their fellow student down the town's main street.

As Jason told me this story, he said that halfway down the street, a hint of sanity returned, and he reached a critical point where he had to ask himself what he was going to do if he caught the child.

Jason never did catch the young boy on his bike that day. However, the story shows how high levels of stress can impair our judgment and inhibit our ability to make good decisions, both in our personal and professional lives.

Stress does not come from the situations we experience, but rather from our emotional reaction to the situation.

It is significant to note that stress does not come from the situations we experience but rather from our emotional reaction to the situation. Feelings such as anger, sadness, or fear immediately activate the body's stress response. Stress only becomes negative when an individual endures constant challenges without moments of relief. Taking on extra tasks, working late, and having increased responsibilities can push you toward distress. When stress is prolonged, it can lead to burnout. Many people are not even aware that this is taking place, and they continue to push themselves. They ignore the physical signs of stress, such as body aches and pains, until it manifests as something more serious.

One study revealed that 75 to 90 per cent of all doctors' office visits are for stress-related ailments and complaints (Goldberg, 2007). Symptoms include high blood-pressure, headaches, indigestion, ulcers, fatigue, and physical weakness.

Chronic stress occurs when your body is in a constant state of stress. Many professionals believe that this causes changes in the immune system, and may contribute to diseases such as cancer, diabetes, stroke, and heart disease.

Heart disease continues to be a leading killer in our society. While stress does not directly cause heart disease, the ways that we manage stress certainly play a role. People may choose to consume alcohol, smoke cigarettes, or eat unhealthy foods in an effort to combat stress. These coping methods may lead to high blood pressure and damage the artery walls, putting the individual at risk for heart disease.

Everyone responds to stress differently, and your ability to tolerate stress depends on many factors, including everything from genetics and environment to your overall view of life. Once an individual is able to recognize that stress is having a negative impact on their life, they are in a position to change their behaviours.

Stress will always be a part of our lives to some degree. However, we determine how we manage the stressors around us.

"Working hard for something we don't care about is called stress.
Working hard for something we love is called passion."

— Simon Sinek

ADDRESSING STRESS IN THE WORKPLACE

Stress vs. Performance

The Yerkes-Dodson Law states that we all require some level of stress to motivate us to perform well in our day-to-day lives, but too much stress will impair our ability to perform at all. This law is demonstrated in the chart below.

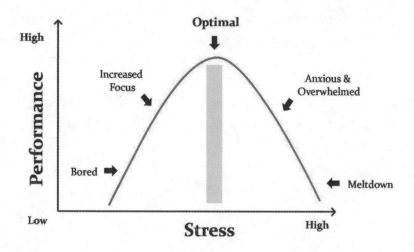

As stress increases, performance will also increase, and we will eventually reach our optimal stress level. It is important to note that this optimal point is different for everyone. Performance actually peaks under moderate levels of stress, and as long as stress is not prolonged, it is harmless. This moderate level of stress keeps the brain alert while enhancing concentration and focus. This is where people often feel as though they are "in the zone."

However, if stress levels continue to increase, performance will then decrease. Once performance begins to decline, an individual typically tries harder, which only increases their stress level and causes performance to decrease even further. This can create feelings of anxiety, frustration, and anger. In this time of distress, an individual's IQ is also significantly impaired.

Thompson (2007) studied the effects of stress on people in leadership roles and discovered that too much stress results in a drop in cognitive ability, including IQ and Emotional Intelligence (i.e. a person's ability to successfully perceive and manage their emotions). Combine this with a heightened emotional state, and it is easy to see how one can be incapable of making appropriate leadership decisions while under a great deal of stress.

A Stressful Environment

The workplace has the potential to create significant challenges, and one of these begins even before entering the employer's doors. In 2010, the General Social Survey, which collects data on the living conditions and well-being of Canadians, revealed that it takes Canadian workers an average of 26 minutes to get to work on a typical day. Many individuals find commuting to be a source of extreme stress and frustration, and they bring this negative energy with them into the workplace.

Other key factors that create stress in the workplace include lack of resources or training, long work hours, job security, and excessive workloads. Any one of these challenges can transform the workplace into a highly stressful environment.

Work-related stress is the response that people may have when presented with work demands and pressures that do not match their knowledge and abilities, and that challenge their ability to cope.

According to the 2010 General Social Survey, 27 per cent of Canadian workers described their day-to-day lives as being highly stressful. In other words, nearly four million adult workers experience a high level of stress on a daily basis. Interestingly, the majority of these workers identified work as being the main source of their stress.

Employers are becoming painfully aware that they are losing productivity as a direct result of employee stress in the forms of absenteeism, reduced work output, and increased disability claims.

These issues are not unique to Canada and can be found in workplaces across the world. Some employers recognize work stress as a health and safety hazard, and take a proactive approach to these issues. For example, Sweden has legislation that requires work conditions to be adapted to an individual worker's physical and psychological circumstances. Workers also have the opportunity to participate in planning their work (UFCW Canada, 2015).

Although there is no legislation that acknowledges work stress as a health and safety hazard in Canada, employers are realizing that work-life balance and a rewarding career for employees are key ingredients to operating a successful business. Thankfully, employers are starting to proactively address the issue of stress in their companies.

3 Tools to Manage Stress in the Workplace

When employees are given the proper tools to manage workplace stress, employers will see the benefits in their workplaces. It is fair to assume that every workplace comes with its own unique set of challenges. If we can agree that experiencing some form of stress is inevitable, then it is essential to plan accordingly and proactively.

While the tools presented below could certainly apply to all areas where stress is present, the following techniques may be used specifically in the workplace.

1. Identify the Stressor

Situations that cause you to experience stress are referred to as stressors. As a counsellor and teacher, I am often told by others that they are stressed. Yet, when I ask them what exactly is causing them to experience stress, they have a difficult time identifying their stressor. Until you know the answer to this question, it is going to be difficult to move forward.

In order to manage your stressors, you must first identify the cause of your stress—and your thoughts, feelings, and reactions to it. Once you do this, you will be in a better position to manage your stress.

Take time to reflect on the following six questions:

1. What situations cause you to experience the most stress?
2. Who was present?
3. How did you feel?
4. How did you react?
5. What could you have done differently?
6. What level of control did you have over the situation?

Many areas of life are beyond our control, especially the behaviour of the people around us. Rather than exerting energy on what is around you, direct your attention back to yourself. How much control do you actually have over the current situation?

It is well known that it is not stress itself that causes problems, but rather your reaction to it. If you can't avoid a stressful situation, try to alter it. To move forward, identify what you can do so the problem doesn't present itself again in the future. Often this involves changing the way you communicate with others.

2. Manage Your Time

When I ask people to identify one thing they need more of, most people will respond with "time." If you are unable to manage your time, it is difficult to manage anything else.

Poor time management can certainly lead to an increase in stress. When you have too much on your plate and are running behind, it is difficult to remain calm and focused. If you take the time to create a plan, you are in a better position to manage your stress.

Below are four suggestions to make the most of your time:

1. Set realistic goals and deadlines.
2. Learn how to say "no."
3. Only work on one project at a time.
4. Protect your time.

If you are anything like me, you may find it difficult to focus on the task at hand for any length of time. Research has revealed that modern workers are interrupted seven times per hour, and distracted up to 2.1 hours per day (Goudreau, 2013). Disruptions may include everything from a phone call or text message to an unexpected visitor.

To enhance your production and increase your chances of success, think about what you can do to control your environment. For example, you could close the door, turn off the phones, take a deep breath, and begin with your first priority.

You should be aware of what you can and cannot do with the time that you have. Avoid setting yourself up for disappointment by demanding perfection or filling your plate with more than you can manage. Act as your own advocate, and establish your boundaries so that you can best manage your time. If you have a deadline in one hour, communicate to those around you up front that you have a deadline and that you would appreciate not being disturbed for that time period. When you explain your situation in advance to those around you, most of the time your coworkers will respect your needs and save their comments or questions for when you're finished.

3. Just Relax

When was the last time you allowed yourself a vacation? CBC News (2013) revealed that Canada ranks third last among economically advanced countries in the amount of paid vacation time it guarantees its workers. For the most part, Canada mandates 10 days of paid vacation for its workers per year of employment. France has the highest levels of paid vacation with 30 days. Meanwhile, the United States—where workers are not guaranteed any paid vacation time by law—came in last place.

BBC News (2015) discovered that 40 per cent of workers in the United States who *were* entitled to vacation days did not take all of these days. They said they were afraid they would not have a job to return to if they took time off.

It is essential to step back at some point and take time to recharge. If you regularly take the time to relax, you will be in a much better position to handle life's stressors when they appear.

For some individuals, the idea of relaxing means lying on the couch to watch TV or going for a drive. While these are possible ways to relax at home, these activities typically cannot be performed in the workplace. Additionally, these behaviours do very little to directly reduce any negative effects of stress.

Below are two simple and effective tools that can allow you to relax when under stress in the workplace:

1. Progressive muscle relaxation
2. Mindful breathing

Before initiating these activities in the workplace, do your best to minimize your distractions. This might mean closing your door or turning off any electronics that would interfere with your ability to focus. Loosen any clothing, kick off your shoes, and allow yourself to simply relax.

Progressive Muscle Relaxation

In times of stress, our muscles become tense because the body is always on guard, ready to fight off any potential threat. Muscle tension can be associated with jaw pain, headaches, and various other aches and pains.

Progressive muscle relaxation involves both the tensing and relaxing of successive muscle groups.

Before engaging in this particular exercise, it is recommended that you consult with your doctor to ensure that you do not have a history of any injuries that could be aggravated by tensing muscles.

Below is a possible sequence of muscle groups:

1.	Right foot	7.	Buttocks
2.	Left foot	8.	Abdomen
3.	Right calf	9.	Right hand
4.	Left calf	10.	Left hand
5.	Right thigh	11.	Shoulders
6.	Left thigh	12.	Face

Starting with number 1, contract the muscles in your right foot and hold for 7 to 10 seconds. Then, release and direct your attention to the sensation of your muscle as it relaxes. Next, bring your focus to the left foot, and repeat the same sequence. You can select whichever muscle groups you feel are most beneficial. People typically progress from the bottom of the body to the top.

When repeated over time, you will become familiar with what tension and relaxation feel like in different parts of your body. This awareness allows you to identify the first signs of stress, and respond proactively and accordingly. Once the body relaxes, the mind will soon follow.

Mindful Breathing

When we are under stress, we often experience shortness of breath. This is one of the body's reactions to a perceived threat. Taking the time to "just breathe" will help minimize your body's fight or flight response, and bring you back into a state of balance. The act of breathing will physically force your body to slow down.

Mind-body practices like yoga, meditation, and deep breathing exercises can put the body into a physiological state of deep relaxation that alters the way it reacts to stress. This state can actually counter the negative effects of stress for people with health conditions such as anxiety or hypertension (Gregoire, 2013).

The way that people view meditation has changed over the years. It does not have to mean chanting a series of *oms* for 45 minutes. Rather, meditation is now seen as a way to center yourself while focusing on your breath.

Breathing is the number one way to reduce stress. In the workplace, you can simply take a step back from the task at hand, and breathe. Taking three deep breaths into the depths of your belly will help reduce your response to stress.

Breathe in through the nose while envisioning the air as white light entering your lungs and expanding throughout your entire body. Exhale through your mouth, and envision blowing out thick, black, toxic smoke. Try to imagine that this black smoke is all the stress leaving your body.

Breathing should be performed in a slow and controlled manner. It may feel unnatural to begin with, but with practice it will become easier and more natural. Inhale slowly for four seconds, hold for two seconds, then exhale slowly for another four seconds. Wait a few seconds before repeating the process. Ideally you should aim for six to eight cycles per minute, although this will depend on what you find to be the most comfortable.

Many people struggle to get the breath past the chest and into the abdomen. This is especially true for individuals who have endured various forms of trauma. For the best results, place one hand on your stomach, and take a deep breath, making sure that your hand rises with each one.

Again, the key is to breathe deeply into the abdomen. This will ensure that you get as much oxygen as possible. With the increase in oxygen, tension will dissipate and anxiety will decrease.

By taking the time to engage in breathing exercises, you can improve cognitive functioning, enhance creative thinking, and also increase productivity.

How Do You Respond to A Colleague in Distress?

How do you respond when you observe someone who appears to be experiencing a significant amount of stress or pain?

My mental health issues began at the age of 17. My academic grades quickly slid downhill while I began to deviate from leadership roles. I went from taking immense pride in my physical and mental well-being, to being wildly intrigued by alcohol and cigarettes.

What message do we get when nobody approaches us when we are in pain?

Teachers observed these changes in me. They expressed their concerns to my parents, but not one teacher approached me. What is the message we get when nobody approaches us when we are in pain? That nobody cares. It can be difficult to care about ourselves if we feel that no one else cares about us. Did my teachers care? Yes! I know they did. But they did not know how to approach me.

Scenario:

You have worked with Kim for years. Recently, she has been displaying some behaviours that are concerning to you. She will often arrive late, leave early, and take extended breaks. While she used to be well groomed, she now appears dishevelled and unkempt. Her moods are also unpredictable. One moment she is outgoing and friendly, while the next she is short-tempered and isolates herself.

It is evident that Kim's mind does not seem to be on her work. She makes mistakes while doing tasks she has performed for years. As a result, you are starting to feel unsafe around her. How do you respond?

If you do nothing, the following six outcomes can occur:

1. Kim's condition will worsen.
2. You and your co-workers will be forced to pick up the slack.
3. Team morale will decrease.
4. Productivity will decrease.
5. Company costs will increase.
6. Both your safety and the safety of others will be at stake.

When faced with the pain of others, people struggle with how to respond. The majority of us care, but many of us have no idea how to express our concern. As a result, we may sit idly by and never address the situation in a proactive way.

Silence speaks loudly, and these situations require a response. The reality is that there *is* no perfect response, and rarely can a response actually make the situation better. Nevertheless, sometimes just listening and sharing your appreciation that they took the time to talk with you is enough to validate their pain.

Big Ears

I recall going through one particularly challenging time in my life. Realizing I could no longer manage the fight on my own, I found the courage to reach out to a good friend. I gave him a glimpse of my painful reality and then waited for his response. His eyes darted back and forth, he patted me on the shoulder three times, and then quickly said, "You are a good guy, Al, you will figure it out." Then he ran like the wind, as though he couldn't wait to escape his discomfort.

Clearly my pain made him uncomfortable and he was not sure how to respond. I firmly believe that nobody needs to be fixed, but the value of been seen and heard is immeasurable. Men in particular often have a desire to fix things when they believe that something requires attention. Personally, I don't measure up to this stereotype. I know that cars have four tires and that is about the extent of my knowledge. However, I do still feel that innate need to fix situations around me. My good wife will often tell me, "Al, I don't need you to fix me, I just need you to listen."

When we see someone in pain, we can simply approach them and say something like, "I'm not trying to be nosy, but I just wanted to let you know that I'm concerned. If you ever need to talk, I'm here to listen."

We all want to be seen and we all want to be heard. The simple statement above says, "I see you and I acknowledge your pain." And your invitation to listen provides them with the potential to feel heard.

The individual may not accept your invitation immediately, but they may walk through your door days or even months later. If they do take this step, it is essential that you drop what you are doing and actively listen. Recognize that this person just took a courageous step forward, and failure to acknowledge their courage could cause them to take two steps backwards.

I am convinced that everyone wants to express their pain, but many simply do not know how to do so. In an effort to keep their wall of defenses up, I have heard clients say, "You can't possibly understand what I have gone through!"

If we respond with, "Oh yes, I can. I went through abuse, mental illness, divorce, etc.," we are moving in the wrong direction. It is not about us, it is about *them*. Their last piece of the wall falls when we respond with four simple words: "Help me to understand."

Just like that, you will see the person let their guard down, and the words will spill out. The moment they are able to release some of their darkness, healing will begin. From that point forward, all you need to do is listen.

The problem is that the act of listening is often easier said than done. Countless individuals lack the skill to listen. I mean really listen. As a child, I sat in countless classrooms and studied subjects such as math, science and history. But schools never offered a class on listening.

Our biggest challenge is that we often do not listen to understand, but rather to respond. For example, perhaps someone just shared with you the news that their loved one was recently diagnosed with cancer. Rather than listening, you begin to tell them that your mom also had cancer. While your intentions might be great, again remember that it is not about you, but rather them.

Think about some of your recent conversations. How much time did you spend talking? How much time did you spend listening?

> There is a distinct difference between *listening* and *hearing*.

There is a distinct difference between *listening* and *hearing*. Listening takes energy. It requires actively paying attention to each word that the other person says while trying to understand the feelings that exist behind the words. Listening demonstrates that you are trying to understand the other's experiences.

The act of listening is one of the greatest skills we can possess. When we listen, we are telling the other person that what they are saying is important. Feeling heard can actually enhance our overall sense of self-worth.

Listening is a skill, and when there is motivation to listen, it can certainly be taught. In the workplace, small gestures have the ability to influence the overall environment. More importantly, you have the ability to change someone's life.

The Value of Feeling Valued

This desire to be valued is one of our basic needs, and the need to be valued guides our behaviours from an early age. Kids find out quickly what they have to do to feel valued. Perhaps that means receiving straight A's at school, excelling in extracurricular activities, or being an active member of the community.

I always enjoy the opportunity to hear my friend and respected leader, Val Desjarlais, share her wisdom. During one particular community event on her reserve, Val announced that in the past year she had placed star blankets on eight different coffins.

In Val's culture, a star blanket is presented to demonstrate great respect, honour, and admiration for that person. The presentation of a blanket is like wrapping the respect and admiration of everyone in the community around the person, both physically and spiritually.

Standing in front of her people, Val stated that she never wanted to see another star blanket on a coffin. She asked a very simple question,"Why would we not honour individuals while they are still alive?"

Too often, our society only recognizes people after they die. How often do you acknowledge the people around you? When was the last time you expressed your appreciation for someone, or thanked an individual for a job well done?

Think about how you feel when someone takes the time to send a compliment your way. When recognized for a task well done, we are empowered and motivated to do more.

In the workplace, if an employee feels valued, three outcomes will naturally occur:

1. The individual will feel empowered to work harder.
2. Team morale will be heightened.
3. There will be an overall increase in productivity.

When we have the power to make someone feel good about themselves and motivate them to perform to the best of their ability, why would we not take a few moments out of our day to do just that?

If You Don't Enjoy Your Job, Start Looking

A significant amount of our lives is spent working. If your work is causing you so much stress that it takes away from your ability to enjoy life, then it might be a good idea to seek new employment.

I listened to one man struggle to find the words to express how much he dreaded walking through the doors of his workplace. After one particularly long day at the office, he walked out to the parking lot but could not find his car. He sat down in the middle of the parking lot, cried, and experienced his first meltdown. Thankfully, this served as the catalyst for him to seek alternate employment. Within a few weeks he began a new job filled with both passion and excitement.

Not everyone has the courage or ability to walk away from their job, even if it is a major source of stress. People can feel stuck and may not believe they can find happiness elsewhere. Financial reasons or fear of change may also play into their decision to remain.

My friend's sister, Laura, was approaching her 70th birthday, and was counting down her remaining days of work. Laura had less than two years before she could retire in order to receive a pension. She did not enjoy her job and experienced many moments of high stress. However, she took comfort knowing that she would be able to enjoy life and take time for herself in the near future.

One morning, while at work, Laura experienced chest pain. Concerned, she went to the hospital for further examination. The doctors found some complications, and, sadly, two weeks later she passed away due to heart failure. Life is interesting—you just never know what tomorrow will bring. Sometimes the only way your body can make you slow down is to shut down.

I recall one occasion when I was driving home after a memorable speaking engagement. As I navigated my way through the beautiful prairie landscape, I listened to Dr. Wayne Dyer's audio book, *10 Secrets for Success and Inner Peace*. One of his phrases stood out like black on white, and demanded my full attention.

Dyer said, "Whatever your passion is, I promise you can make a living doing it." It was in that moment that I decided I would make speaking the focus of my career. With four kids, a wife, a cat, two dogs, and a few tanks of fish, I could not jump in with both feet. However, with the support of my wife, I began to dedicate more time and effort on making this passion of mine a reality.

If you are passionate about your work, it does not seem like work. Dyer sold me on that simple but profound idea.

"When I was five years old, my mother always told me that happiness was the key to life. When I went to school, they asked me what I wanted to be when I grew up. I wrote down 'happy.' They told me I didn't understand the assignment, and I told them they didn't understand life."

— JOHN LENNON

ARE YOU HAPPY?

Life Is Hard

I was speaking with a young man who shared with me that he had recently begun using illicit drugs. I asked him what he gained through this behaviour, and he told me that he found life to be incredibly challenging and that drugs allowed him to get through each day. After asking him what part of life he found challenging, he replied with three words: "All of it."

I certainly do not dispute the fact that life is hard. While life's challenges provide us with the opportunity to grow, many of us feel like we are being stretched too thin. Countless people are in pain, and many are uncertain how to manage it. Nonetheless, my personal and professional experiences have demonstrated that healing will never take place through the use of substances or self-injurious behaviours.

When faced with a particular challenge, it is easy to grow impatient. We often want what we want *now*. If we begin a project that is challenging in nature, we often wish that it were simply done already. When we are in pain, we often wish for the pain to pass. In the same way, while we are always ready for the reward, we are not always ready for the work.

Lucky is a documentary about the American lottery, and it follows some of the industry's biggest winners. Not surprisingly, the majority of the lottery winners drastically changed their lifestyles following their sudden financial wealth. While some bought private jets and fast cars, others bought mansions and large estates.

Meanwhile, one middle-aged man went against the grain. Six months after winning the lottery he made two purchases: diamond earrings for his wife and a modest Volvo. When questioned about his actions, he explained that when you are not wealthy, you can afford all these fantasies about what you would do if you won the lottery. However, after winning, he found that the desire for all of those things quickly disappeared. He no longer wanted a Lamborghini. This man realized very quickly that he enjoyed the possessions that he worked for the most. Not only did he work to own his house, but he also had no desire to move from the place where his kids had grown up.

Possessions handed to us on a platter do not hold the same value as something obtained through blood, sweat, and tears. Think about your first job. Remember when you received your first paycheck and you had the freedom to spend it as you saw fit? Perhaps you even put some of the money away into savings for a future purchase.

Envision a teenager who balances school with his first part-time job at a fast food restaurant. After more than two years, he is finally able to save enough money to purchase his first vehicle. Sure, the vehicle is pushing 20 years old and is peppered with noticeable rust spots. However, it is his first car, and he loves it. Why? Because he earned it, and he knew exactly what it took to get that car.

Now imagine a teenager who has just received the keys to a brand new car from his parents. This adolescent never had to flip a burger, mop any floors, or lift a finger to receive the car. The internal value of this vehicle simply cannot be compared to that of the other teenager who saved up his hard-earned cash from his first job.

In January 2016, a Powerball lottery jackpot reached a record 1.6 billion dollars. Millions of people purchased tickets in the hopes of winning big. One in five Americans believes that their best chance of getting rich is by winning the lottery, not through hard work. The actual odds of winning that Powerball lottery were one in 292.2 million. The odds of being struck by lightning are one in 1.19 million. You do the math.

Where Are You Going?

What do you want out of life?

If you don't know where you are going, how will you ever arrive at your destination? Without this insight, you can only accidentally stumble upon any successes.

If you find yourself lacking motivation, it has nothing to do with laziness. Rather, what you lack is a specific focus. The clearer you are about what you want, the more your brain knows exactly how to get there.

As a counsellor, I am well aware of the fact that I cannot force my clients to change unless they themselves have an internal desire to change. Sometimes all it takes to inspire and motivate yourself to want something better is to take a good look at where you are.

Look at the image below and put yourself in the shoes of the person standing at a fork in the road:

Now, without thinking, answer a simple *yes* or *no* to the following two questions:

1. Are you happy?
2. Are your behaviours getting you what you want out of life?

If you answered "yes" to both questions, you are on the correct path that will lead to a fulfilling and prosperous life. If your answer to either of these questions was "no," then something has to change to reach your desired outcome.

In the same way that death is inevitable, so is change. We often fear change because of the way it makes us feel. While change causes us discomfort, it also provides the opportunity to grow.

Let's suppose you responded "no" to one of the questions. The path to the right represents the current path you are on at this moment. If you change nothing, you will experience a level of comfort on this familiar path, but it will not provide you with true happiness.

Meanwhile, the path to the left represents the journey that awaits you following change. Making a conscious decision to change will force you to leave familiar patterns. Will you stumble? Will you fall? Yes. But you will also *grow*. More importantly, you will be closer to becoming the person you were meant to be.

Moving Through Change

In the early stages of change, there will likely be moments when you have to "fake it until you make it." To fight old behaviours you will need to rewire your brain, and the only way to create new connections is through real experience.

Imagine that a blizzard has left more than two feet of snow on the ground. Standing at the front door, you stare at your car parked on the street. You step outside, and as you walk toward your car, you create a path. Where do you think you will walk the next time you leave home?

The more you walk up and down that path, the more trampled it becomes, and the harder it will be to leave it. Should you ever decide to take a different path, it will require great effort to break through the snow and create a new one. And yet, the more you walk in this new direction, the more a new pathway will form.

For change to take place, you must first believe that change is possible. You must not only want to change, you must also be ready for it.

In the face of change, our minds can sometimes create a fear that is worse than reality. To combat this fear, ask yourself, "What is the worst thing that can happen?" Imagine it—walk through the middle of these fears. For example, if you have to give a speech, your greatest fear might be that your nerves will cause your knees to buckle, and you will end up rolling right off the stage. Whatever the case may be, ask yourself if you are able to deal with it. The majority of the time, you will discover that you have the strength to persevere through your worst-case scenario.

On the other hand, challenge your brain to think about the complete opposite outcome. Ask yourself, "What is the best thing that could happen?" You might be pleasantly surprised at how it unfolds. While giving that speech, your words might resonate with someone and restore some light to their time of darkness. That person might approach you later and applaud the courage it took for you to deliver your message.

And be realistic. Ask yourself, "What is most likely to happen?"

These three questions will allow you to regain control over the situation, and provide you with the strength to face the challenge in front of you head-on.

Changing from Within

We all want to feel like we have the freedom to choose. In addition, we all need to experience a level of control.

I spent many years working at an in-patient treatment centre for people who were struggling with addictions. On several occasions, an adolescent expressed frustration and anger over the fact that their parents made them come to treatment.

I would always challenge this belief, and remind them that the choice was still theirs. I informed them that they could walk out the door at any moment. Sure, there might be consequences for that action from an outside source (such as a family member), but they still possessed the freedom to choose.

Like everyone else, they just want that feeling of power, and the sense of being in control. Some clients would exercise the right to walk out the door. More often than not, a few minutes later there would be a knock at the door and they would return.

However, what was different was that they knew they could leave, and this gave them a renewed sense of control. The fact that they then stayed for themselves had a significant impact on their ability to learn and increased their potential for change.

Change is only real when someone acts on change themselves, for themselves. Many years ago I had the privilege of volunteering at a special care home. The property was home to serene grounds that provided residents the opportunity to be surrounded by nature. In the spring, boxes of soil arrived for those who were interested in gardening. This activity was an outlet that allowed them to connect with something outside of themselves while also enhancing their overall sense of purpose.

The idea of gardening intrigued Scott, one of the men I regularly visited. Scott had two boxes designated for him, and he took his time thinking about what he wanted to plant in each. After acquiring some seeds and small plants, it was time to begin. As we approached the boxes of soil, Scott asked if I would be willing to do the planting for him. He explained that it would be challenging for him, considering that he was in a wheelchair.

Sure, I could have performed those tasks for Scott. However, this was his project. If I planted them, it would have taken away from his experience, and there would be less motivation for him to return to care for the plants daily. The act of doing it himself would create internal pride, and allow for a future sense of accomplishment. It was Scott who needed to dig the holes, plant the seeds, and water the plants. Scott was more than capable of doing these tasks. He just needed some encouragement.

Some of my clients always ask for various forms of assistance. Perhaps they need to schedule an appointment with another professional. It would be easy for me to make the call for them, but then there is no opportunity for them to take control and experience a sense of pride in their accomplishments. Doing something for someone who is capable of doing it on their own sends the message that we don't believe they are strong enough to do it. While we can open doors for those around us, we certainly don't need to hold their hand and walk through the door with them.

In the same way, I believe that everyone possesses the ability to answer their own questions. The right questions just need to be asked. When we think for ourselves and solve our own problems, we become empowered.

The moment you take ownership and responsibility for your life, you regain control.

The moment you take ownership and responsibility for your own life, you regain control. This is your life, and nobody else's. There will always be people who will try to impede you on your journey, and challenge your ability to evolve and grow. Perhaps they will attempt to force their beliefs on you, believing that they know what is best for you.

On numerous occasions, I have spoken with a parent who will say something like, "My child is making all the wrong choices!" But who is to differentiate between right and wrong? The decisions that the child is making might be right for what they are supposed to learn at that very moment in their life.

Sometimes, people want to intervene on behalf of those who they believe are making poor decisions. While there is a time and place for this, I believe that each person ultimately needs to find their own way.

Failing to Succeed

Jeff Bezos, founder and CEO of Amazon.com, took a unique approach when he launched his delivery service, AmazonFresh. Rather than choosing people who had experienced success in a similar business, he hired individuals who had failed.

Bezos believed that these people brought something to the table that was worth much more than high grades, awards, and an impressive resumé: they brought invaluable insight gained in overcoming their recent challenges. These individuals thought outside the box and were willing to take risks without letting the fear of failure stand in their way. They never perceived failure as a negative but rather asked themselves what they could learn from that particular experience. Bezos's approach paid off, and his business has become extremely successful in recent years.

Failure is inevitable; it is a natural part of our lives. But our perception of failure will determine the way we handle it.

Gloria, a former student, stared failure in the face more than most while she pursued her dreams of post-secondary education. Between 1980 and 2004, she enrolled and dropped out of university a staggering 15 times. It was not a lack of effort on her part, but she was simply unable to complete a program.

It was not until 2001 that an Aboriginal support worker approached Gloria to explore why she was unable to achieve academic success. After convincing her to get an assessment, it became evident that Gloria had a learning disability. While this insight provided an explanation for her challenges, she was still unable to complete a program. After 15 years of university, Gloria walked away with only two years of credits.

In 2013, Gloria entered my classroom, determined to be an addictions counsellor. She took advantage of the various resources available and fought her way through the program. At the age of 55, Gloria marched triumphantly across the stage and received her diploma. Her strong skill set immediately led to employment as a case manager. Today, she empowers others to dig deep and persevere through their own personal challenges.

Failure is subjective in nature. Only you have the power to decide whether something is viewed as a failure. While the educational institutions and instructors labelled Gloria a failure, she understood that she was anything but. She never let herself be defined by her failures and never gave up.

In Greek mythology, Achilles' mother dipped him into a magical river to make her son invincible. But because she held Achilles by the heel, it prevented the powerful water from protecting this small area, and it was the only part of his body that remained vulnerable.

As Achilles grew into adulthood, he was feared by many. He possessed skills of courage, bravery, honour, and strength. He was a skilled fighter who became a great hero of the Trojan War. He was only killed when an arrow penetrated his heel.

Like this Greek warrior, we all possess an Achilles' heel. This is what keeps us vulnerable, humble, and essentially human. Everyone carries different fears, which often remain hidden. There are those who are challenged by greed, anxiety, or various forms of mental health problems. Diseases such as cancer can present themselves to prove that life is indeed fragile.

Our Achilles' heel can serve as a good reminder that we are vulnerable, and it is this vulnerability that helps keep us grounded. Rather than seeing it as a weakness, though, we can turn it into a strength. Once we identify our areas of vulnerability, we possess a greater awareness of ourselves.

Only a small portion of our growth comes from our successes; most of our growth stems from our failures. Instead of teaching people how to succeed, perhaps we need to do a better job of teaching people how to fail. Furthermore, we need to get rid of the word *failure* altogether, and simply call it *experience*.

4

GO WITHIN OR GO WITHOUT

The Mask

The advancement of technology has brought society to a place where it seems as though someone is always watching. Our actions can be tracked by everything from the cameras that decorate the walls of banks to the random citizen who records various events around them on their cell phone. Interestingly, the camera lens only captures what takes place on the surface. For many, when the door is closed or the lights are off, a different reality exists.

Every morning my students and I gather around in a circle and engage in a daily reading. I was intrigued by one reading in particular—the words challenged the reader to think about how they would respond if they were approached by someone who whispered, "They know..."

As you reflect on this question, is there anything that immediately comes to your mind?

Who knows?
How much do they know?

How do you act when nobody is watching? The world used to be my stage, and I put on a wonderful act for all to see. On the outside, people saw a young man who was president of the student representative council, athlete of the year, and the recipient of countless academic awards. Even as an active addict I received a national scholarship as an outstanding community citizen. I accepted this award with feelings of both sadness and guilt. I wanted to scream, "This is all an act!" Sadly, I never knew how to talk about my painful reality. I didn't use my voice in times of need because I feared judgment. It was both exhausting and draining.

Caitlyn Jenner, formerly known as Bruce Jenner, spent years suffering in silence. Recently she has emerged from the shadows, and her personal journey has been placed in the international spotlight. Caitlyn spent the majority of her life battling with her identity in ways that few can fully understand.

Ironically, the name "Bruce Jenner" became attached to an ideal of masculinity in 1976 after she won an Olympic gold medal in the men's decathlon. After nearly 40 years in hiding, Caitlyn removed her mask and publicly identified herself as transgender. Finally, she was able to be her true self.

Caitlyn was the 2015 recipient of the Arthur Ashe Award for Courage. Not surprisingly, this award came with controversy. One online post showed an image of Caitlyn Jenner sitting beside a war veteran who was missing both legs. At the top of the image was a caption that read, "What is real courage?"

Like many things in life, courage is subjective. Nobody can fully understand the actual amount of courage required except that particular individual. Personally, I struggle to understand why Caitlyn's experience has to be compared to anything else at all. It is hers and hers alone.

During Caitlyn's acceptance speech, she alluded to the thousands of teenagers who are coming to terms with who they are. She made it clear that these individuals should not have to be subjected to bullying or words of condemnation from others. Unfortunately, toxic words propel countless people to consider suicide because they fear being who they are. This is a true tragedy.

I am reminded of a parable about a little boy who had a bad temper.

His father gave him a bag of nails and told him that every time he lost his temper, he must hammer a nail into the back of the fence.

On the first day, the boy had driven 37 nails into the fence. Over the next few weeks, as he learned to control his anger, the number of nails hammered in gradually dwindled down day by day. The boy found that it was easier to hold his temper than to drive those nails into the fence. Finally the day came when he didn't lose his temper at all.

After sharing this with his father, the father suggested that the boy now pull out one nail for each day that he was able to hold his temper. The days passed and the young boy was finally able to tell his father that all the nails were gone.

The father took his son by the hand and led him to the fence. He said, "You have done well, my son, but look at the holes in the fence. The fence will never be the same. Understand that when you say things that hurt others, they leave scars. It won't matter how many times you say 'I'm sorry,' the wound is still there. You must understand that a verbal wound is just as damaging as a physical one."

This parable reminds us that we need to taste our words before we spit them out. It is often easier for us to look outward, and yet *We need to taste our words before we spit them out.* we need to start looking inward. None of us can fully understand another's path. It is imperative that we create a society where people can simply be who they are: a society in which people will not face judgment when they remove their masks.

Caitlyn is trying to promote a very simple idea. She is asking each of us to accept people for who they are, and to accept each other's differences. Don't we all want to know that we are enough just the way we are? Caitlyn's act of courage will empower others to remove all kinds of masks.

How Often Do You Wear a Mask?

Have you ever opened your eyes in the morning only to be greeted by some form of internal pain? Perhaps there was a recent loss in your life, a strained relationship, or a financial hardship that you are working through.

Some days you are able to stay in the confines of your home, while on other days you are painfully aware that you must engage with society. To ensure that you can face the day, you put on your mask, take a deep breath, and walk out the door. Meanwhile, you stuff your internal pain deep within.

Whether your life circumstances cause you to be surrounded by complete strangers, peers, or colleagues at work, you display your radiant smile for all to see. The moment that someone acknowledges your presence, they shout out the familiar phrase, "Good morning! How are you doing?" And like a well-programmed robot, your response is automatic. Through a forced smile you squeeze out the word, "Good!" Their smile matches yours and life goes on.

This idea of pasting a smile on the outside is instilled within us from an early age. I always dreaded the day that my mom announced it was time for our annual family picture. Reluctantly, I would put on my best clothes while ensuring that my hair was combed to perfection. Our family got into our car like we were a fragile work of art, doing our best not to wrinkle our clothes or mess up our hair.

Once in front of the photographer, I fought to maintain my statue-like pose. When the photographer was finally content with all of our individual poses, the next word was always the same, "Smile!"

So there we were, smiling until our cheeks were sore in the hopes that Mom could later find at least one picture that met her standards. The whole thing seemed like we wanted to show our friends and family members that we were, in fact, happy. Now, I am not implying that we *weren't* happy, but it seemed like we were just posing on a stage for all to see.

This pattern continues throughout various aspects of our lives. We upload images to social media sites like Facebook or Instagram that showcase moments of contentment. We carefully select clothes that match recent trends, and might even attempt to showcase our cars and homes. These forms of public display can also sometimes serve as masks.

So what purpose do these masks serve?

We select different masks depending on how we want to be perceived, or to match a particular situation. When we meet someone new, we might hide who we are because we fear that we will be criticized or not be accepted. We often wear a mask when we want to hide our true selves. Perhaps we are afraid that others will perceive us to be weak or vulnerable.

There are times when we have no choice but to wear a mask. In the workplace, you might be expected to constantly wear a smile and radiate positive energy to ensure high quality service or customer satisfaction. In my own career as a teacher and counsellor, it is sometimes necessary to temporarily hide any internal pain so that I can focus on the needs of those in front of me.

The key is to understand when we are wearing a mask and to identify the purpose that it is serving. The goal is to remove our masks as much as possible so we can be our authentic selves. If we stay true to who we are, we will not be met with suspicion. When we lead a life of honesty and integrity, there is nothing to hide.

It takes a lot of energy to be someone that we are not. But it takes no energy to simply be who we are.

> *The goal is to remove our masks as much as possible so we can be our authentic selves.*

Who Am I?

"What are these scars from?" she asked.
"They're battle wounds." I replied.
She looked at me for a long time.
"Who were you battling?"
"Myself."

—Unknown Author

I believe that the greatest battle that we will ever fight is the one with ourselves. If we can conquer that, then we will achieve true peace.

How would you respond if a stranger approached you and asked, "Who are you?"

Many people would likely look like a deer caught in headlights if asked that question, and struggle to provide a response. The truth is that many people have no idea who they really are. In fact, many of us go six feet under without having the foggiest notion. You might know everything about a famous celebrity, or your partner, but know very little about yourself.

We live in a non-stop world, and it is easy to get swallowed up by everything taking place around us. Our attention can be taken hostage by our education, career, children, or our attempts to attain greater financial wealth.

In our haste and distraction, we are rarely alone with ourselves. Even at home after a day out in society, we often find ourselves bonding to some form of technology. Silence can provoke a sense of discomfort and fear. To combat this uncomfortable feeling, we may fill the room with music or sound waves spilling from the TV. And so we do not spend time with ourselves, and do not take time to go within.

In the same way, addiction also serves as a way to live outside of ourselves. Whether someone turns toward a substance, food, sex, or work, it is still an escape that prevents them from having to be with themselves.

While working a night shift at an in-patient addiction treatment center, a female client came into my office and stood in front of my desk.

"Can't sleep?" I asked her.

"No," she answered, somewhat sheepishly. "Can you do me a favour?"

"Sure. What do you need?"

"Can you go to Wikipedia on your computer and search the meaning of my name?"

I smiled and replied, "I can do that, but can I ask why?"

Her eyes were suddenly filled with a deep sadness. Her tone softened, and while she stared at the floor, she said, "Because I am trying to figure out who I am."

Active addiction prevents an individual from knowing who they really are. In her case, further discussion revealed that she had started using drugs at the age of 15. Chronologically, she was now 24, but her drug use had delayed her emotional development. She missed out on her wandering years. This prevented her from the opportunity to grow and the chance to get to know herself. In the field of addictions, we often refer to this as the "Peter Pan Syndrome."

A person will never understand their own identity if they don't search for it. It requires looking into the past, and exploring everything from childhood to the present. You must identify the scripts you were given, look at the values that were instilled, and dissect the countless teachings received.

This process of discovery is kind of like going out for coffee with yourself. Ask questions. What motivates you? What brings you happiness?

To some degree, I believe that we all exercise behaviours that are addictive in nature. We all attempt to avoid pain and discomfort, and replace it with some form of pleasure. We all yearn to find happiness, and each of us goes about this in our own unique way. Countless individuals desperately seek outside themselves for the very answers that can only be found within.

How many times have you heard someone say, "I will be happy when…"? This fill-in-the-blank might be getting a promotion, a faster car, a spouse, or a place to call home. But while a form of happiness might be felt upon the arrival of these events or possessions, attaining those things does not guarantee ongoing happiness.

In one of my workshops, participants are asked to navigate their way through an activity called the "Who Am I Wheel." There are many variations, but I choose to examine eight different areas: I want, I need, I like, I love, I dislike, I wish, I fear, and I am. Participants are required to identify four points about themselves under each of the eight areas within a five-minute time span *(see p. 50)*.

There are always some participants who initially scoff at this idea, believing that it is so simple that it is a complete waste of their time. After the exercise, I ask those present to raise their hands if they found this activity to be more difficult than they initially thought. Every single time,

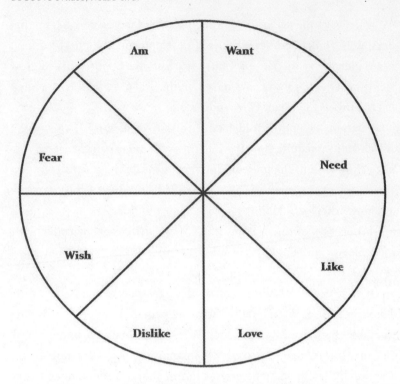

the majority of hands reach for the sky. When asked why they found it so difficult, many respond saying they really don't know who they are. For many, this is a startling revelation—and it should be.

The Teachings of a Turtle

The moment you look outside of yourself for the answers you are seeking, you give your power away. When you go within, you will find all of your answers.

It is the turtle that teaches us the importance of going within. From this sacred space you are able to reach the very core of your being. Suddenly, you find yourself in a position of strength, and nobody can lead you to do or become anything that you do not want to do or be. From here, you can manifest and create your own reality.

There are countless resources on the topic of self-care that exist with the hope that people can lead more fulfilling lives. You can be given the best research and the most extensive list of tools, but there is no incentive to take care of yourself if you do not find yourself to be of value. You can tell someone that they are valuable, loved, and unique, but to actively apply tools of self-care, they need to believe these concepts from within.

The turtle also reminds us to slow down. We seem to be hard-wired to want what we want *now*. When we send a text message or an e-mail, we desire an immediate response. If we order new furniture from the store, we want it delivered as soon as possible.

Many people maintain the belief that if they were not busy throughout their day, then they were not productive. Interestingly, this idea of being busy is often associated with a sense of importance. If you have a long to-do list, countless people to see, or e-mails to send, then you must be important, right?

I have always had a busy mind. Both the volume and frequency of noise can be deafening, and I never used to know which voice to listen to. Naturally, I would go with the voice that fought for my attention the most—the voice that screamed the loudest. In time I discovered that it was not the loudest voice that deserved my attention, but rather the quietest. I recognized that the only way to hear and connect with this voice was through my own silence.

If we operate in a hasty manner, we often act without honouring our feelings. Have you ever been unsure about a particular situation, and rather than waiting, you took action? Once the situation unfolded, did you regret your decision to act?

If you are not sure what to do, do nothing.

If you are not sure what to do, do nothing. Our gut constantly provides us with strong and accurate information. This is where we hold our intuition. Rather than acting when unsure, wait for clarity. Then you can move forward, confident in your decision.

When we slow down, we are able to live in the moment. We can remove our tunnel vision and actually see what is taking place all around us, and also what is taking place within. And it's not just about slowing down, but also about being mindful of what we are doing.

My three-year-old son teaches me how to be present in the moment.

On one occasion in our backyard, he stopped what he was doing and crouched down on the ground, mesmerized by something in the thick green grass. I walked closer and saw a ladybug lying on its back, its legs kicking the air in desperation. In no time, this determined little bug managed to flip itself upright and began navigating its way through the grass. The whole time my son just watched, fascinated by what was taking place right in front of him.

The elderly seem to share this same ability to stay in the now. Perhaps this is why such a special relationship exists between young and old. These age groups are able to live in the moment with the understanding that life is precious, limited, and valuable.

Some people become stuck in the past or even the future, but this squeezes out the present. All that we have is the present moment. If you find yourself moving too quickly through your life, take a step back. Stop what you are doing, feel your feet on the ground, breathe, and take in your surroundings.

Some people spend their entire lives searching for something that has existed inside of them the entire time. If you are uncertain where you are headed, just remember the teachings of a turtle: go within and slow down.

> *"Don't hold onto anger, hurt, or pain. They steal your energy and keep you from love."*
>
> — LEO BUSCAGLIA

5

EMOTIONS THAT FEED STRESS

The Toxins of Anger

There is a great parable about two dogs. A woman observed these two dogs go into the same room at separate times. The first dog made its exit from the room wagging its tail, while the second dog left the same room growling.

The woman was perplexed as to what was in the room that would cause these two dogs to have such different reactions. She went into the room, and to her surprise, found herself surrounded by hundreds of mirrors. She realized that the first dog had been greeted by hundreds of dogs who welcomed its arrival with warmth and love. The second dog, on the other hand, was greeted by hundreds of hostile and aggressive dogs. This story demonstrates a simple message: what we see on the outside is actually a reflection of what is taking place on the inside.

When we have anger deep within, it can change the way we view both the people and the world around us. Anger has the ability to make a simple situation *Holding onto anger is like drinking poison and expecting the other person to die.* manifest into one that causes extreme stress. Buddha reminds us that holding onto anger is like drinking poison and expecting the other person to die.

A friend of mine, Sean, had intense anger toward a man who had sexually abused him as a child. This anger had grown over the years, and was now becoming toxic. His internal rage was preventing him from enjoying the world around him. He understood that in order for him to experience even an element of peace, this emotion needed to be released.

This insight motivated him to make an appointment with a counsellor. Halfway through the session the counsellor asked Sean, "If I gave you a gun right now, and your perpetrator walked through the door this very moment, would you shoot him?"

Let's just pretend that this man actually did walk through the door, and Sean did decide to shoot him. Would Sean's pain remain?

Internal pain does not simply vanish through a single external act. No matter what form of violence Sean directed toward his perpetrator, his emotional pain would remain. When you have anger or hate in your heart, it gets stored in your body. Over time, this can lead to sickness. The mind also rents out head space to this anger, and can be taken hostage. Some people are willing to let others rent out their mind space for free.

A teacher asked all her students to bring a bag of potatoes to school. The teacher instructed the students to think about all the people they held a grudge toward, whom they struggled to forgive. Once they had compiled their list, they were asked to carve those names into the potatoes, one name per potato.

Over the next week the students were expected to carry around their personalized bag of potatoes everywhere they went. The bag sat on their laps on the morning bus ride. They carried their bags with them during recess, and set it beside their beds at night.

It did not take long for these students to realize how much of an inconvenience this bag was. It was starting to really weigh them down. It also became evident that the people whose names were inscribed into these potatoes were not affected in the least.

Eventually, the students understood the meaning behind the exercise, and discovered that there was no payoff for carrying around emotional burdens. As a class, the students then sought out ways to release this unnecessary weight. The class realized that they no longer wanted to hold onto their anger. They were left with a choice. They could live with the anger that was stealing their peace, or they could choose to surrender and release it.

Looking Beneath the Anger

Have you ever encountered someone you just couldn't tolerate? It is not unusual to have an individual in your life that causes you some discomfort. Perhaps it is their passive-aggressive approach, immaturity, or negative energy that forces you to keep your distance.

You fight to enjoy your day, but any pleasurable experience seems overshadowed by their presence. You might even blame them for ruining your day. Maybe you even try to schedule your day around that person, ensuring that you have as minimal contact with this individual as possible.

This individual may be a family member or a co-worker. Regardless, you always feel that a break from this person would be good for your overall health. Does that insight ever cause you to pray for that person to be sick or absent so you can get that break? I have been guilty of this a few times myself.

Even if your prayer was answered, their absence was likely short-lived. Have you ever stood back and asked yourself what it was about that particular person that provoked such a negative emotional response within you?

I have often wondered if some of my more challenging former clients and students stayed up late at night thinking of new ways to test my patience and push me to my breaking point.

But when I took a step back and reflected on my own experiences, my perspective changed. I learned that the stress I experienced actually had very little to do with those who challenged me most. What caused me to experience the most discomfort was the fact that I lacked the tools to deal with those particular people. I realized that, at times, they even displayed character traits that I did not like in myself, everything from defiance and stubbornness to shame and anger.

Interestingly enough, the people who have caused me to experience the most stress have always become some of my greatest teachers. If I had avoided or ignored their challenges, not only would I have done a disservice to them, it would also have impeded my own personal growth.

Anger vs. Compassion

Over the years, I have discovered that the clients who were the most aggressive, or the ones who acted out the most, were always the ones who were in the most pain. The problem was that they did not possess the tools to manage their pain.

My friend, John, was bullied repeatedly throughout his childhood by a boy named Jeremy. Growing up in a small town, Jeremy seemed to be around every corner, and constantly made John's life a living hell. Over the years, John's anger toward this boy evolved into a toxic hatred. Finally, graduation came and he left the small town, grateful that he no longer had to deal with Jeremy.

More than 20 years later, John received some information that caused him to shift his entire perspective. He discovered that Jeremy used to go home every day after school only to fall victim to his father's abuse. In fact, the father also abused Jeremy's sister. Sadly, the abuse was so severe and had such a lasting impact that Jeremy's sister took her own life.

John suddenly felt rather conflicted. Was he supposed to just let go of all his anger and resentment toward his childhood bully?

Clearly, Jeremy had been in a lot of pain as a child, and he felt the need to project his own pain onto others. Essentially, Jeremy was attempting to regain a sense of control while living in a home environment that was very much out of his control.

Children learn behaviours. I believe that every child enters the world pure and innocent. I do not believe that a single infant arrives in this world a racist. In the same way, no child is born with an internal desire to inflict pain on another human being.

Now, I am certainly not justifying Jeremy's behaviour. His actions had a significant impact on John's life. However, what I do know is that when we approach situations with anger, we will certainly end up with more anger. With this response, we move in the wrong direction.

A more proactive approach is to seek the underlying cause of the pain. As soon as we approach these situations with compassion, the entire outcome changes and we can move forward in a healthier way.

I was taught that the only time you look down on someone is when you are trying to help them up. The next time someone is lashing out, or causing you to experience immense amounts of stress, take a step back and shift your perspective. Remind yourself that you have no idea what drives that individual's behaviours. If they are full of anger, ask yourself what could have happened in their life for them to carry so much rage. What could you potentially learn from this person and situation?

As difficult as it can be, I encourage you to see the person and not the behaviour. Take the time to get to know who they are. Listen to their story and find out what makes them tick.

Empathy is a strong emotional tool. It requires you to remove your own glasses and wear those of the other person. Now, you stand in their shoes and see the world through their eyes. You stand with their beliefs and all the experiences that brought them to the present moment. Empathy provides a deeper level of understanding.

Shame

Shame is a powerful emotion and its magnitude is often underestimated. If guilt can be understood by, "I made a mistake," shame can be understood by, "I *am* a mistake."

Shame is debilitating and can affect everything from self-worth and body image to relationships and the ability to have a successful career. The person can feel as though shame defines who they are, keeping them from reaching their full potential.

Shame can be intense to the point that people feel the need to deflect and focus on things outside themselves. One of the most common cover-ups of shame is perfectionism. The moment someone does something that is perceived as wrong, they become vulnerable to experiencing shame. The individual might engage in people-pleasing behaviours and strive to ensure that everyone around them is happy at all times. But this is an impossible challenge—we all know that it is unrealistic to please everyone around us.

Abuse is the most common cause of immense feelings of shame. Abuse comes in several forms, including physical, mental, emotional, or sexual. Victims are powerless and helpless during these traumatic events. This loss of control can continue long after the events are over.

The first thing that someone observes when they see you is your body. If your body has been violated in any way, you may feel defective in the eyes of others. Bones and bruises will heal, but the emotional damage can last a lifetime. Shame changes how you see yourself and how you behave toward others.

We are social beings, and we were born to have relationships with other people. The problem is that when you have been abused, you commonly push away those who get too close. It's not that you don't want to let people in, but there is fear of trust, pain, and the possibility that they will discover the secret that lies at the root of your shame.

Not knowing how to manage this internal pain can cause people to act out their pain externally. Subconsciously, you may want to hurt others because you want to hurt yourself. It can be a great challenge to remove bricks from your wall to let your guard down. It is a slow process to regain levels of trust and to let people into your life.

Sadly, many people are victims of abuse, but unless they proactively seek healing, they will always remain a victim. By focusing on recovery instead of the abuse itself, you will be one step closer to healing.

Healing

Regardless of the challenge, many people want to be restored and wish to be whole again. Healing cannot be found outside oneself. Rather, healing and transformation is only possible by changing one's perspective from within.

If you give yourself permission to sit with your pain, you will allow yourself to have a better understanding of it, and the place from which it stems. With this insight, you can determine whether you need additional supports to assist you through the pain.

It is both challenging and painful to uncover old wounds. But with bold courage, you can dig deep and move through the pain while freeing up space. When the darkness is brought into the light, it cannot survive. Light will always triumph over darkness. Until we deal with our darkness, we can never truly stand in the light.

Until we deal with our darkness, we can never truly stand in the light.

When the decision to progress toward healing is made, some people view it as an event, linear in nature, resembling the image below.

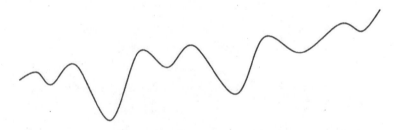

However, these individuals quickly realize that instead of being an event, healing is more of a process. The path toward healing is not linear, but consists of many highs and lows.

Healing provides us with the opportunity to get to know ourselves. For some, healing is drastic, and for others it is smooth. The process of healing is unique to you, and cannot be compared to anyone else. There is no timeline to heal, and you must progress at your own pace. As the saying goes, "You can't eat an elephant in one bite." Take a small bite out of the elephant, deal with what you can, then put it away for later. Eventually it gets to a manageable size and you can put it away for good.

To move forward, we need to acknowledge our pain, and honour this pain by facing it head-on. The first step is acknowledging that there is something inside of you that demands your attention. Acknowledgment is simply the mind's understanding that something is taking place. Only once you arrive at the point where you realize that what you are doing is not working can you make a change.

Acceptance means putting the body where the head is. It is through acceptance that you can be catapulted into action. The only way to heal is to see yourself as you are. Healing requires looking into your past but not getting stuck there.

Since I was a kid, I have had a fascination with eagles.' While all other birds fly away from a storm, an eagle flies directly into it. They carefully position themselves to take advantage of the incoming winds that eventually lift them high above the storm. In the same way we can use our storms to rise to a higher level. When we persevere and make it through personal challenges, we arrive with a different perspective. Suddenly, the way that we view the world around us changes.

Time and time again I have heard people say, "I would not take away any of my personal hardships because they have made me the person I am today." It is evident that they have received something positive from these experiences, and they have also grown. If you have made a similar statement in the past, hold tightly to this belief the next time you are faced with a personal challenge. It is this belief that will assist you in your time of darkness. After all, if life were all unicorns and rainbows, we would not appreciate what we have. If we were always in a state of happiness, we would lack a sense of appreciation and gratitude.

This understanding has the ability to change the way we view personal challenges. Rather than waiting for the storm to pass, know that you will grow and be blessed by being able to see life through a different lens when it is all said and done. A wise woman once told me:

> *You cannot go forward until you have looked into your past. Otherwise you will always have something holding you back. Like a bow, it will keep pulling you back. Only once you take the time to go within and do the work can you truly be released. When you let go, it will catapult you forward.*

Talking Facilitates Healing

I believe that everyone wants to talk about their pain, wants to be free from it, but not everyone knows how to achieve this. Perhaps they fear judgment, other people's reactions, or that once they speak about the issue it becomes "real" and triggers negative emotions. Although talking can be one of the first steps to healing, the key is not to simply talk about your feelings, but to feel your feelings.

The key is not to simply talk about your feelings, but to feel your feelings.

I spent one morning speaking with students between the ages of 12 and 15 in a small northern community. Many of these students were still painfully aware of a tragic event that had taken place just over a year earlier. While biking near a bridge, one of their peers was struck and killed by a drunk driver.

Following my presentation, all the students but one filed out. In front of me was a young girl, her head resting on top of her desk, face down. Clearly, the presentation had provoked an emotional response.

"Do you want to talk?" I asked gently.

"No," she responded, and her head remained down.

I made eye contact with the teacher and was grateful when he kindly left the room, allowing the two of us to share the space.

I tried again, "How about now?"

She shrugged. This was a good sign, and I knew we were moving in the right direction.

I grabbed a chair and set it down beside her desk. I said nothing and let my presence show her that I was all ears if she needed to talk.

A few seconds later, she said, "I am afraid to talk."

"Why?" I asked.

"Because I am afraid to cry."

"And why are you so afraid to cry?"

"Because I don't like feeling sad," she replied.

I decided to respond with a question. "Have you ever felt better after a cry?"

She thought for a moment, then quietly said, "Yes." She lifted her head from the desk, looked at me in the eyes, and as the first tear left her eye, she whispered, "I miss my friend."

Just like that the door was opened. I spent the next few minutes simply listening to her while providing the odd comment. Before leaving, she wrapped her small pinky finger around mine, and pinky-promised that she would continue to talk about her pain to people she trusted. I left knowing that healing had begun in that classroom.

Letting Go

If something is starting to feel out of control, then it probably is. It is important to understand that the issue does not lie in the situation itself, but rather in the fact that you are choosing to hold onto that situation for so long. There are countless circumstances around us that we have no control over. We have no power over another person's thoughts, attitudes, or actions. What we do have power over is how we respond to them.

Everyone deserves the freedom to live life on their own terms. The more we focus on what lies within our control, the more power we have. From this place, we can focus on our journey while maintaining a level of inner peace.

I never had a brother, but my best friend, Justin, was as close to a brother that I could ever have imagined. He was the best man at my wedding, and he delivered a powerful and emotional speech outlining our strong and unique bond. Just over a year later, I delivered a similar message at his funeral. Justin needed to escape from an internal pain that he viewed as permanent, and died by suicide.

We have no power over another person's thoughts, attitudes, or actions.

On the one-year anniversary of his passing, I travelled to his gravesite to reflect. My loving wife had previously made a frame for me that was filled with different photos of me and my friend. When I got there, I set this frame on the ground in front of me. Immediately, it fell from its upright position. Unfazed, I gently picked the frame up off the ground, wiped off some debris, and again placed it in front of me. Again, it fell down. It wasn't even windy.

Slightly frustrated, I repeated this process. Just as before, it fell down once more. At that point I got mad. I stood up, spread my arms open wide, and screamed, "What's going on?"

Clear as day, I received one word: "Enough."

It was in that moment that I understood. I had spent so much time the previous year thinking about what I could have done, what I should have done, that it caused me to miss out on my own journey. It was at this moment that I was able to let go, and I took a big step toward healing.

Letting go means that you choose to release your grip on something that is preventing you from being able to enjoy your life. There is a process for letting go and it always involves allowing yourself to feel.

One of my clients in the addiction treatment centre released his anger through the act of writing. This middle-aged man had endured horrific abuse. As a young child he was forced to attend a residential school. He shared how his culture had been stripped from him, and how he was taught to hate not only his culture but also himself. Additionally, he was the victim of several forms of abuse. For decades he had been storing immense rage toward one nun in particular. Even though she had long since died, his pain remained.

This man took the time and energy to be with his pain and wrote a letter to the nun. The pen gave him the freedom to say anything he wanted to her. He expressed all his feelings and slowly began to unleash his anger.

Following this emotional release, he wanted closure. Together, we stood outside and burned the letter. Through the smoke, he released the power and control that the nun had held over him for all those years.

Creating a Safe Space

Sometimes we are able to manage the pain on our own. But if we are injured on a deep emotional level, the chances that we can manage it on our own are very slim. In these cases it is essential to reach out for help.

This can be a huge hurdle for many, especially for those who are in the helping profession, everyone from nurses and doctors to counsellors and teachers. This kind of pain is a double-edged sword for them because although these individuals know what they are supposed to do, they may lack the ability to apply it in their own lives. There is also a fear of damaging their reputation, and the potential of losing their career.

In order to work with others you need to clean up your own mess first, so to speak. If you don't have it in you to give, step back and let someone else do it. You must take care of yourself to be able to take care of others. As crazy as it seems, the world will go on without you as you take the time to step back and focus your attention on yourself.

Asking for help is not a weakness but rather a strength.

Asking for help is not a weakness but rather a strength. Acting on the resources available is one of the greatest gifts we can give ourselves. It teaches us to live, and that life can be enjoyable.

Sometimes it can seem as though we are the only ones enduring a particular struggle. That thought causes us to feel alone in our fight. The moment you are with someone who has had similar experiences, a weight is lifted. Two powerful emotions that greatly assist an individual's healing are compassion and understanding.

There are numerous support groups that bring together people who face similar challenges in their lives, from grief and loss to mental health or substance abuse issues. A 12-step program such as Alcoholics Anonymous is a prime example.

Sometimes I hear a client say, "Well, where I am from there are no 12-step meetings." My response is always the same. "Start one." There is no reason why an individual can't start a group of their own with any theme that connects two or more people. When you create a safe space around a common theme, it is only a matter of time before people come.

We all yearn to be met with compassion and to be free from judgment. When people come together in this way, it is inevitable that healing will take place. These spaces allow people to hear their own stories through others and slowly, shame slips away. In this way, we allow ourselves the opportunity to release some of our darkness while making more room for light. These groups are proof that talking truly does assist in the process of healing.

If a tragedy strikes at your place of work, I guarantee that people are feeling the emotions. Where do they go with these feelings? A safe place can be created to offer people the simple opportunity to come together and talk.

People need space to share and to see the faces of others in order to validate the fact that they are not alone. There is comfort in the recognition of shared emotion when someone else comes forward to express what you feel too. And you quickly realize that they are just like you, and that you are not alone.

"Life isn't happening to you; life is responding to you."

— Rhonda Byrne

LIVING IN BALANCE

Mental Wellness

Over recent years, a strong emphasis has been placed on the issue of mental illness in our society. While I strongly believe we must continue to bring this prevalent issue into the light, I feel as though we spend too much time talking about mental illness, and not enough time talking about mental wellness.

The World Health Organization (2014) defines mental wellness as, "A state of well-being in which the individual realizes his or her own potential, can cope with the normal stresses of life, and is able to make a contribution to his or her own community."

Western culture often perceives mental health to be focused solely on the "mental" aspect. On the other hand, First Nations cultures view mental health as the balance and harmony within and among the four aspects of human nature: physical, mental, emotional, and spiritual. The Medicine Wheel reflects these four parts of our being. This philosophy is based on balance and requires an individual to focus an equal amount of attention on each of the four areas. If even one of these areas is out of balance, the person is out of balance.

In Western culture, schools and workplaces tend to focus primarily on the mental and physical components. However, to achieve true balance it is imperative that we closely examine emotional and spiritual aspects as well.

1. Mental

You were not born to give up in the face of adversity. Rather, you were born resilient. You possess the strength to perse- *You were born resilient.* vere through any challenges that present themselves.

I recently listened to one of my students share how she was held back from Grade 1 three times. Tears rolled down her cheeks as she relived her initial struggles to understand why she was slower than her peers. Then the tears suddenly stopped flowing and a look of sheer determination and strength swept over her face. Her tone changed and she proudly spoke about her ability to persevere through her challenges and her determination to receive a college diploma.

Do you see yourself as someone who can't catch a break in life or do you see yourself as someone who can overcome all obstacles?

How you think can have a profound effect on your overall well-being. If you want to determine how healthy you are, pay attention to your thoughts. Thousands of thoughts run through your mind every day, so be careful how you speak to yourself. Your thoughts directly relate to how you feel about yourself, and ultimately how you act.

Self-talk refers to the way that we communicate with ourselves. For example, if you make a mistake, do you tell yourself that you are stupid or should have known better, or do you sit back and think about what you can learn from the experience? Your personal messages slip into your subconscious where they are recorded as either positive or negative. Your body will believe whatever messages it receives and will act accordingly.

Negative thoughts can prevent you from enjoying life and impede your ability to grow. If you catch yourself delivering these negative messages, write them down and think about how you can turn them into positives. In time, positive self-talk will evolve into an automatic response.

2. Physical

In order to lead a fulfilling life, we need to respect and take care of our bodies. When battling life's stressors, it can be quite tempting to engage in habits that do not benefit our physical well-being.

I used to smoke cigarettes in an effort to manage my stress. My grandmother would often voice her displeasure and would gently remind me that if I was supposed to smoke God would have made me with a chimney.

To take care of your body it is important to drink plenty of water and eat a well-balanced diet. Healthy food choices have actually been found to counteract the impact of stress on your body.

Adequate sleep is also vital for your overall health and well-being. The National Sleep Foundation (2015) recommends that teenagers get between 8 to 10 hours of sleep per night, while adults require 7 to 9 hours of sleep. In a world where there never seem to be enough hours in a day, the majority of people do not receive enough sleep.

The Division of Sleep Medicine at Harvard Medical School explains that a lack of sleep can result in a number of consequences. In the short term, it can affect judgment, mood, and the ability to learn and retain information. In the long term, chronic sleep deprivation may lead to obesity, diabetes, cardiovascular disease, and even early mortality.

Not surprisingly, sleep loss can lead to accidents and injuries on the job. Sleep deprivation was actually a factor in some of the biggest disasters in history. In 1989, a third mate fell asleep at the wheel, causing the Exxon Valdez oil spill. This became the second largest oil spill in the history of the United States causing 11 million gallons of oil to spill into the open ocean. Meanwhile, investigators ruled that sleep deprivation was behind the 1986 nuclear meltdown at Chernobyl after engineers had worked 13 hours or more (Division of Sleep Medicine, 2007).

Regular physical activity is a well-known way to feel better, have more energy, and even live longer. The Public Health Agency of Canada (2011) advises that physical activity has been shown to reduce the risk of over 25 chronic conditions, including coronary heart disease, stroke, breast cancer, and Type 2 diabetes. Clearly, physical activity is one of the best things we can do for our health.

3. Emotional

It is important to be aware of your emotions, how you respond to them, and ultimately how you release them. When you are balanced emotionally, you are able to manage stress, adapt to change, and are in a position to maintain control over your life.

An emotion is created by any reaction, whether it is real or imagined. Feelings are neither good nor bad, they just simply are. As mentioned earlier, many people do a tremendous job of deflecting their true feelings and focusing their attention outwards as opposed to inwards.

Feelings are neither good nor bad, they just simply are.

We do not have the ability to turn off our emotions like a faucet. Left unmanaged, feelings do not just disappear. Rather, they are buried alive. If you are sad because a good friend recently passed away, but you strive to avoid feelings of grief by acting as though the tragedy never took place, the sadness will remain.

It is not so much the pain itself that taxes us, but rather the energy we exert trying to resist the pain. We consume much more energy trying to store and suppress the pain than it would take to confront it head on. These emotions are stored in our tissues, muscles, and organs. We can only suppress so much—eventually all emotions will make their way to the surface.

Pay attention to where you feel the emotion, and what your body is telling you. One woman shared that her fear was located in her throat and upper chest. She discovered that the reason she held her breath when she was afraid was because she wanted to cry but didn't feel safe to do so. Before this realization, she constantly had sore throats and tonsillitis. As she dealt with her issues, these symptoms began to disappear. Today, if she ever gets a sore throat, she pays attention to what is taking place in her life.

Feelings don't just happen. There is always a reason behind each emotion. When an emotion surfaces, it may not only be connected to the present situation, but also tied to an event that took place in the past. Individuals who go into a fit of instant rage likely need to examine what is causing such an explosive outburst.

One father watched as his young son left for a nearby hill on his bike. This young boy climbed the hill and proceeded to ride back down. As he approached the bottom, the boy became aware that he would not be able to stop under his own power. To his absolute terror, he was heading directly for a parked car. A split second later both he and his shiny red bike crashed into the parked car.

Having seen the entire event unfold, the father arrived at the scene less than a minute later. He towered over his son, who now lay in a heap of wreckage at his feet. He saw tears streaming down his son's face and watched as his son struggled to free himself from the handlebars wrapped around his left leg.

The father was suddenly catapulted into a state of absolute rage. He bent over this fragile child and began to repeatedly punch his son in the face, screaming for him to stop crying.

The question is why?

I believe that everything in that father wanted to take his son's pain away. I am convinced that he wanted nothing more than to be able to nurture his own flesh and blood, pick him up, and make him feel better. But this father had no idea how to reach that place within.

I am certainly not justifying his reaction to the situation; his actions are absolutely unacceptable. There is, however, always an underlying force that drives our behaviour. Men are supposed to fix things, but this man lacked the tools to comfort his son because he was never taught how to deal with his own emotions. All he knew was that his son's accident was making him feel an emotion he hated. He hated feeling helpless, sad, and confused. The father believed that the only way for him to stop feeling these uncomfortable emotions was to make his son stop crying.

In a world that can be filled with painful experiences, many boys continue to be conditioned not to cry and to suppress their emotions. These behaviours seem to go against the stereotypical idea of being a "man." Often, when you ask boys to define the meaning of strength, the vast majority immediately make some reference to physical attributes.

Think about entering a room, perhaps your staff room at your place of work, and seeing a woman whose face is buried in her hands while she weeps uncontrollably. Most people would quickly attempt to provide her with some comfort.

But if it were a man weeping, would your immediate response be different?

Most people would be slightly uncomfortable and might arrive at the conclusion that something incredibly traumatic had taken place in the man's life to provoke such an intense reaction.

Boys need to understand that real strength is shown by men who can express all forms of emotion. As men, it is essential that we teach boys to put a voice to their pain, feel their pain, and to release it in a healthy manner.

Once I came home from an exhausting day at work and my oldest son asked how my day had been. I immediately replied with the automatic, "Good," and flashed a smile.

Then I caught myself. My day had not been good. In fact, it had been incredibly frustrating. My son could clearly sense that my verbal response did not meet my physical demeanor. I had just taught him to suppress his true emotions and put on that familiar mask.

I corrected myself. "No. You know what? Today was rather frustrating."

I felt better—not only was I honouring my feelings, but perhaps modelling my true emotions would mean that in the future my son will feel comfortable sharing his own frustrations.

If you can't control your emotional state, everything around you will remain out of control. Feelings need to be examined, understood, and ultimately released. Thank the emotion for what it has taught you, and once it no longer serves you, release it, and let go. If it remains, perhaps there is more to learn.

4. Spiritual

Like many others, I believe that we are spiritual beings having a human experience. I view the body as nothing more than a shell that houses our spirit. This spirit has a desire to live life to the full-est, but the challenges of life can keep this spirit suppressed. To be balanced and whole, each of us needs to form a connection with our spirit.

We are spiritual beings having a human experience.

It is not difficult to believe in something that we can see, touch, feel, taste, and smell. Spirituality, however, is a challenge to our senses. There is nothing tangible to hold, and it requires a belief that can only exist within.

We all possess a deep desire for some form of spirituality, and we all arrive at it in our own way. While some people find spirituality in nature, others may find it within the confines of a church or synagogue. It can be found through an unexpected act of kindness or in the smiling eyes of a complete stranger during times of personal struggle.

Confusion often exists between the ideas of religion and spirituality. Religion can be a way to become more spiritual but it does not have to be part of the process. Spirituality is a personal connection with a higher power.

In a world filled with so many personal beliefs, it is important that we maintain a level of respect for the spiritual connection each person has. Respect the fact that what works for you may not work for another person.

A potential client interested in one of my workshops asked me to meet him for coffee. In our conversation, he asked me to explain my spiritual beliefs. Spirituality is deeply personal, and unless asked di-rectly, I typically never discuss this topic. However, I did my best to ar-ticulate some of my beliefs but stopped when I realized I was being met with resistance. This man immediately began to challenge my beliefs and tried to convince me otherwise. Before we parted ways, he told me that he would pray for me, hoping that I could find what he has found. I know that his intentions were positive, but spirituality is something that must be discovered by each of us. For there to be meaning, spirituality can never be pushed onto us by external force.

We are said to be made of three parts: body, mind, and soul. As stated previously, I believe every one of us enters the world innocent and pure. As we progress through life, we experience a number of hardships and personal pain.

Many of us struggle to meet our eyes in the mirror because we despise the reflection staring back at us, perhaps hating what we have become. Guilt and shame can be overwhelming. Few people want to take an honest look inside themselves because they fear what they will find. But I am convinced that when an individual sorts through the darkness, they will find a soul that is completely spotless. Our minds and bodies can be battered, bruised, and violated, but at no time can the soul ever be damaged. The soul always remains intact and can never be touched.

Our minds and bodies can be battered, bruised and violated, but at no time can the soul ever be damaged.

My personal and professional experiences have shown that this belief is a catalyst for healing. Rather than believing that we are damaged, we can now hold onto something that is precious, pure, and ours alone. This can serve as the light in our darkness, and create a new sense of hope as we progress toward healing.

"The question is not whether life exists after death.
The real question is whether you are alive before death."

—Osho

7

DO YOU WANT TO EXIST
OR DO YOU WANT TO LIVE?

Are You Truly Living?

Life has the potential to pass you by at an incredible speed. It is not difficult to slip into a state of merely existing instead of living. Many people have a tendency to delay action because they believe they will always have tomorrow. But there are no guarantees that tomorrow will ever arrive.

For many, life is linear in nature, and runs on a predictable course as illustrated in the diagram below.

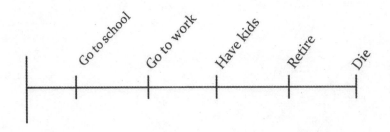

The majority of people will attend school throughout their teenage years, and some might even continue their studies well into their adult years. They will then enter the workforce, perhaps raise a family, retire, and then die. For some, each day becomes something to get through rather than enjoy. You might find yourself stuck in the same meaningless job even if it fails to bring you a sense of fulfillment and happiness. You convince yourself that if you can hold out a few more years, you will be in a better financial position so that you can finally enjoy life.

Perhaps you remain in the same toxic relationship that fails to bring you happiness. Your mind feeds you the false belief that nobody else would want to be with you, or that the current situation is better than being alone. The very thought of being stuck with only yourself may be terrifying. Even the idea of making any significant changes to your life may cause significant stress.

Many people go through the motions but not the emotions. As a result, they rarely become grounded, and they live their lives out of balance.

Imagine someone who keeps one foot on the dock and the other in the boat. He is neither here nor there; he cannot move in any direction. If that person wants to enjoy boating, he is going to have to remove his foot from the dock and commit to getting into the boat. After all, nobody can enjoy a boat ride until the boat has actually launched. Initially, it will be a challenge. He has to figure out where to sit, how to use the oars, and how to guide the boat in the right direction. However, once there is movement, he is on his way.

Unfortunately, many refrain from taking that courageous first step into the boat. There are those who fear failure and there are those who fear success. Some will observe other boats sailing in the distance, and feel resentment or slip into victim mode. They may struggle to understand why others get to enjoy their lives while they don't.

There are those who walk around with a "V" on their foreheads, happy to embrace the role of victim. For years they are consumed with bitterness and a life of merely existence. They exert so much energy *Happiness does not just happen; it must be created.* on what they have lost when they could redirect that energy to getting it back. But the world owes us nothing. If you want something different, if you want to live a different life, only you have the ability to change its course. Happiness does not just happen; it must be created.

Experiencing Life

Recently, I observed a sign outside of a church that read, "The meaning of life is …" Personally, I believe that the purpose of life is to actively experience your own life.

What does it mean to experience life?

Almost daily I see people walking down a sidewalk, eyes fixed on their cell phones. While I am impressed by their ability to navigate safely through crowds of people, I cannot help but feel that they are missing out. Technology has certainly changed how we connect with each other.

Social media, for example, is supposed to connect people, and yet it often seems as though it causes more of a disconnect. You will often see two people out for coffee or a meal, and rather than share a conversation with each another, their focus is on their handheld devices. How many times have you seen something similar? To truly experience life we need to unplug from our electronic devices and see the world around us.

This past summer my wife and I took our kids to the mountains. I used to drive only with the purpose of getting to the next destination, but now I take it all in. During the trip, I found my eyes darting side to side in search of the next waterfall or in hopes of catching a bear slurping from a river. While this also might have something to do with my diagnosis of Attention Deficit Disorder (ADD), I like to think I'd rather not miss out on my surroundings. My wife does her best to manage her anxiety and calmly asks me to please return my attention to the road.

Tools to Live

A Beautiful Prayer

I asked God to take away my habit.
God said, No.
It is not for me to take away, but for you to give up.
I asked God to make my handicapped child whole.
God said, No.
His spirit is whole, his body is only temporary.

I asked God to grant me patience.
God said, No.
Patience is a by-product of tribulations;
*   it isn't granted, it is learned.*
I asked God to give me happiness.
God said, No.
I give you blessings; Happiness is up to you.
I asked God to spare me pain.
God said, No.
Suffering draws you apart from worldly cares
*   and brings you closer to me.*
I asked God to make my spirit grow.
God said, No.
You must grow on your own,
*   but I will prune you to make you fruitful.*
I asked God for all things that I might enjoy life.
God said, No.
I will give you life, so that you may enjoy many things.

—Author Unknown

1. Be Grateful

One of my students told me that she recalled being a young child and sneaking into her mother's room. While snooping around she came across a small book titled *Daily Diary.* Unable to help herself, she opened the book and eagerly turned to the first page.

To her surprise, the page was not written in sentence form but rather in point form. Her eyes scanned a long list that included words like *inner strength, family, yoga,* and *freedom.* She turned to the next page, and found a similar pattern of words. She thumbed through several more pages to discover more of the same. Suddenly, it dawned on her that she was looking at her mother's gratitude journal. While slightly disappointed that there was no juicy gossip to absorb, she was intrigued.

When an individual takes the time to write in a gratitude journal or practice another form of gratitude, the benefits are undeniable.

Physically, an individual who practises gratitude can possess a stronger immune system, lower blood pressure, and experience less aches and pains. Psychological benefits include higher levels of positive emotions, increased energy, and more optimism and happiness. Lastly, gratitude affects people socially by allowing them to be more helpful, generous, and compassionate, while feeling less lonely and isolated (Emmons, 2010).

Thoughts are powerful, and engaging in an activity like writing in a gratitude journal puts deliberate attention on what is going right in our lives as opposed to what's going wrong. In turn, this will change the way that we feel and, ultimately, act. Slowly, your entire perspective of the world around you will become more positive.

The act of giving also provides us with the ability to step outside of ourselves. One of the things I have always admired about my father is his generous spirit. Even immediately following the removal of a brain tumour, this trait remained. From his hospital bed, he looked at me as he winced in pain and said, "After this we are all going to Tim Hortons to get donuts." That painted a nice picture and I built on his vision. "And what kind do you want, Dad?"

The expression on his face changed slightly. "No. Not for us. For all of them," he said, pointing around the room at all the nurses.

The true spirit of giving means giving for the sake of giving with no expectations in return. No public fame, no posting on social media, nothing. This past year a local radio station had a one-day event to raise money for breast cancer. I was blown away when I heard that there was an anonymous donation of $100,000. They key word here is "anonymous." The very fact that this person or company did not need public recognition for their donation serves as a prime example of the true spirit of giving.

At any given point in our lives, there is much to be thankful for. Perspective is everything. Rather than complaining about having to shovel your driveway or weed your garden, be grateful that you have a driveway to shovel and a garden to weed.

2. Set Your Priorities

A father returned home from a long day at work and was greeted by his seven-year-old daughter. She looked up at him, flashed a smile, and asked, "Can I please have five dollars?"

The father was immediately annoyed by the fact that he had just gotten home, and the first thing out of his daughter's mouth was a request for money.

He responded with a firm, "No," and told her to go to her room and play until supper was ready.

After supper, the father retreated to his office where he once again immersed himself in work. Three hours later he left his office and made his way to his daughter's room to say good night.

The father quickly tucked her in, expressed his love, and headed for the door. Just as he was closing the door his daughter softly asked, "How much do you make an hour, Dad?"

Again, the father became agitated. He took a deep breath and firmly said, "It is none of your business. Now go to sleep."

The young girl's eyes began to tear, and the father felt a hint of guilt for his outburst. In an attempt to alleviate some of her pain he said, "I'm sorry. If you really must know, I make 23 dollars an hour."

Instantly, the girl lit up, ran across the room, and picked up her piggy bank. Back on her bed, she poured out all her coins along with a small heap of crumpled bills.

The father watched curiously as his daughter slowly began to count out loud. After surpassing the 23-dollar mark, the girl ran toward her father with a big smile.

Looking up at him, she said, "I have enough money to buy one hour of your time! Can we please do something together tomorrow Daddy? Please?"

It can be all too easy to get wrapped up in our work or in our own needs. This can cause us to neglect those closest to us. It is important to think about your priorities and ensure that you take the time for what you truly value.

3. Love Deeply

John Lennon understood one of our basic needs when he wrote the number one song, "All You Need is Love." Without love, it would be difficult to find meaning in our lives. Feeling love provides us with the opportunity to feel happy and connected to something outside ourselves.

Love can help combat disease, boost immunity, and instantly dissolve all stress (Mahoney, 2011). For some, this feeling of love can come from riding a horse, walking through nature, meditating, playing with the kids, or playing fetch with the dog. If you don't have a pet, research shows that you might want to explore the benefits. Pets can serve as a great companion and even a best friend, and they can also improve your overall health. For almost 25 years research has shown that living with pets can lower blood pressure, decrease anxiety, and boost your immunity. When I return home and open the door it is not my kids or wife that trip over each other to greet me, but rather my two dogs. Many people say that there is nothing like coming home after a stressful day to be greeted at the door by their pet. The stresses of the day instantly disappear (WebMD, 2014).

We were not designed to live in isolation. As human beings, we are all hard-wired to seek out relationships. Many argue that we should not depend or rely on others in order to feel love. Still, the majority of us do. When we love someone, it puts us in a better position to love ourselves. We can reflect on the way that we love others and apply that same love to ourselves. People can only truly love us if we believe that we are lovable in the first place. Every infant enters the world expecting to be nurtured and loved. Sadly, this does not always occur. Abuse and neglect can cause people to feel as though they are unlovable. The truth is that every single individual is worthy of receiving and expressing love.

Smile while you still have teeth! Love can begin through a simple smile. What happens when you smile at those around you? It can be infectious. Allow yourself the freedom to smile, and watch how rapidly the world transforms into a brighter place. It's important to smile while you still have teeth!

4. Learn from Our Greatest Teachers: Children

Consider the characteristics of a young child. They are wild and free, full of passion, excitement, and curiosity. They are constantly on the hunt for the next big adventure. Children have incredible imaginations, and with nothing more than cardboard and some crayons, they can travel to the moon in a spaceship in a matter of minutes.

Last semester I asked my students to create illustrations that demonstrated key events in their lifetime. Several grumbled, complaining that they didn't know how to draw. I asked them to put themselves back in their kindergarten class. If their teacher stood in front of them with a box of brand new crayons and asked, "Who can draw?" how would they respond?

Many children are taught to believe in Santa, the Easter Bunny, and the Tooth Fairy. Then one day they are taught to turn this belief off. At some point each one of us leaves our creative imagination behind as we prepare ourselves for the "real world." In the process, we often lose the ability to play.

While working at an addictions treatment centre, I took a group of youth tobogganing. At first, they all refused to take part, not wanting to lose face in front of their peers. Finally, one brave young soul jumped on a crazy carpet and tore down the hill. His screams of joy were infectious and a few moments later, every single teen was sliding down that hill.

Now, it had been nearly 15 years since I had gotten onto a thin piece of plastic and gone sailing down a hill. But I couldn't resist, and halfway down that hill I felt something come to life within me. It was as if I were finally giving myself permission to play, and I felt a sense of freedom.

Children teach us how to step back from our busy lives and just play. There is something liberating when you throw on some winter gear and build a snow fort. A sense of child-like wonder manifests itself when you build a tree fort or engage in a game of tag. Play is what keeps us young at heart. Taking yourself too seriously will impede your ability to grow and excel.

Journalist and philosopher, Lia Diskin validates the fact that chil-

GOODBYE STRESS, HELLO LIFE!

dren are indeed some of our greatest teachers. At the Festival of Peace in Brazil, Diskin shared a story about an anthropologist who was studying the habits and customs of an African tribe. The anthropologist asked some children from this tribe to participate in a game. He set a basketful of candy at the base of a nearby tree and told the children that whoever got to the basket first would get to keep all of the candy.

After organizing the children behind a line he had drawn on the ground, the anthropologist called, "Go!" To his surprise, all the children joined hands and ran together toward the tree. Once they reached the candy, they all sat down together to enjoy their prize.

Intrigued, the anthropologist asked them why they had run together when one of them could have had all the candy. One of the children answered, "How can one of us be happy if all the others are sad?"

Imagine what our world would look like if we united as one. In a world where there is so much fighting and continuous pain, we can learn a lot from these young leaders.

5. Always Maintain Hope

It has been said by many that hope is the anchor of the soul. In times of despair and darkness, hope is what empowers us to keep fighting.

In Joel Olsteen's book, *It's Your Time*, he writes about an experiment that was conducted on rats. Researchers carefully placed one rat in a pail of water with high sides so that it could not escape. Then they timed how long the rat would keep swimming before it gave up. In a room of complete darkness, that rat swam for just over three minutes.

Researchers then took that same pail and placed it in a room that had a bright ray of light shining through. The rat swam for more than 36 hours.

That study revealed the very idea of hope. If we have light, we fight. As long as you have hope, you can persevere through all obstacles.

As a young adult, I was always on the move and relocated several times. The one constant was that everywhere I lived, I hung the same small picture by my door. With a beautiful sunrise in the background, the words on it read, "No matter how long the night the dawn will break."

In my times of darkness, I leaned on those words of hope. To me it meant that maybe, just maybe, tomorrow would be a better day.

Hope is what reminds us that the darkness will pass.

Nothing is rigid, and nothing is permanent. Hope is what reminds us that the darkness will pass.

6. Move to the Beat of Your Own Drum

While driving with one of my sons, I peered into the rear-view mirror to see why my four-year-old was suddenly so quiet. Usually he would tell me all about our surroundings or ask me random questions.

I saw him tapping his little index finger against the side of his car seat at a tempo that was certainly not in rhythm with the music on the radio. I smiled, thinking that this was the same way he navigated through life. Like other children, he wants to live life on his terms. Sometimes we must remind him that he is not the "boss." Though many would perceive this young child as stubborn, I prefer to use the word determined—just like his old man.

From an early age we are taught to live within a certain set of guidelines. These rules can reflect the norms and expectations society has placed upon us. When we enter school, we are taught to colour inside the lines. What would the response be if a child only coloured outside the lines?

In life, the moment you decide to go outside the lines, you will always be met with opposition. This resistance might come from a family member or an entire community. The way that you think or act outside the box may instill both anxiety and fear within them. It is from this place of fear that they try to influence the way you live your life.

Following high school, my friend Matt wanted to step back from schoolwork and travel the world. His father, however, had different plans. Matt's father wanted him to further his education. In fact, he pushed his desires on Matt so much that Matt finally submitted an application to attend university. After three years of bitterness, Matt completed an arts degree. After graduation, he took his printed degree and threw it at his father, saying, "That was for you. Now it is time to live for me." Matt was in a position of power and always had the ability to choose. But he chose to give his power to his father.

As previously discussed, in any given moment, we all have the ability to choose. When we act in opposition to another's wishes, there might be certain consequences. In Matt's case, if he had decided never to attend university, his father may have raged at Matt for not following his plan and completely distanced himself from his son. However, Matt would then have been living for himself and not for his father.

If you can let go of what others think of you and embrace your own rhythm, you will be rewarded with a renewed spirit and a fulfilling life that is yours, and yours alone.

7. Return to the Journey You Were Meant to Live

This is your journey and yours alone. Some people may get so wrapped up in others' journeys that it takes away from the life they were meant to lead in the first place. For some this may be a partner, sibling, friend, or child.

A young man presented his mother with a gift on her birthday. It was a Willow Tree sculpture of a mother holding her child by the hands as the child learns how to walk. She picked out the perfect spot in her office, and it stayed on the window ledge for years to come.

Her son began to face several challenges, and during this time she entered the room to discover that this precious gift had fallen off the ledge and now lay broken on the floor. The crack in the ceramic caused the little boy to no longer be attached to the mother. Delicately, she picked up the pieces. Placing them on a table, she attempted to glue them back together. Despite her best efforts, a visible crack remained in both of the mother's arms.

Later that evening, she again took a look at the sculpture. She felt deep sadness over the damage. But then she suddenly saw the figure in a whole new light. She realized that when a mother is blessed with a child, it is not hers to carry alone—she will crack with the weight. The child needs to be set free so he can be all that he is meant to be.

That night, she set her child free. She understood that he needed to live life and heal in a way that only he knew and understood to be true for him. She trusted that he would be given the love, grace, and courage he needed. She let go with hope and unconditional love, and turned her focus to her own journey.

My uncle shared with me that he remembered being a little kid, standing on the train tracks and looking toward the horizon to the point where the tracks disappeared. He always wondered where the tracks went from there.

The Navajo First Nation believes that we are placed on earth to learn and to teach. Once we have accomplished our duty, our spirit is ready and we leave. For the Navajo, life is a journey of the spirit and the ultimate goal is to complete our assigned task.

I believe that we each have an assigned task. There is something that exists within each of us that did not exist until we arrived here on earth. If we do not live our purpose, we miss out on fulfilling our legacy.

The very fact that you are reading this means that you have unfinished business. If that were not the case, your higher power (however you perceive it: God, Creator, Allah, Buddha, etc.) would say, "Let's go."

I imagine sitting at a table across from the Creator before I was born. The Creator gave me a long checklist and told me that these were the tasks and lessons I was supposed to learn and teach in my life. I reviewed it, signed on the dotted line, and left, ready to experience my life.

I believe that when we start to deviate from this plan, there will be some form of intervention. Perhaps we will suddenly be involved in an accident, or perhaps become ill in an effort to slow us down and get us back on track. Maybe this life event will put us in a hospital bed. At this moment we are made to slow down and spend time with ourselves. Suddenly there are few distractions and we are challenged to explore the relationship we have with ourselves. We might also ask some of the larger life questions, like what our purpose is.

For many of us, life's purpose is to serve humanity and help others in some way. I have heard several visionaries express the idea that we are happiest when we give our lives away. While I agree that one of the greatest purposes in life can be to serve others, the key is to also serve

GOODBYE STRESS, HELLO LIFE!

ourselves. It is imperative that you don't allow yourself to get so caught up in everything around you that you forget to take care of your own needs. Remember that you are number one.

On our holiday last summer my wife and I were enjoying a hike through the mountains when we both heard some rustling in a near-by bush. While she was wondering what was going on, I was already headed in the other direction. It would be fair to say that she was not impressed by my reaction. For some reason, she was of the opinion that I was supposed to protect her.

I attempted to explain to her that I was just trying to take care of number one: me. I never did tell her that the very reason I wear running shoes is because if we ever do see a bear, I know that I can outrun her. I suspect she would not be amused with my logic anyway.

When I ask people to identify what is important to them, I hear answers like "the success of my kids," "a good job," "my partner," "wealth," or "my health." But the reality is that everything and everyone around us can disappear at any given moment. Relationships will end and people will die. You, however, are stuck with yourself. Yet, if you can learn to enjoy your own company, you will never truly be alone.

We all need to find meaning in our lives. We need something that gives us the motivation to get out of bed in the morning. I believe that everyone possesses something unique inside them that cannot be duplicated by anyone else. To find this purpose, it is essential to slow down and go within. It is there you will find the very answer that has existed since the day you were born.

References

CHAPTER 1

American Heart Association (2014) *Stress and Heart Health*. Retrieved July 24, 2015 from http://www.heart.org/HEARTORG/GettingHealthy/StressManagement/HowDoesStressA ffectYou/Stress-and-Heart-Health_UCM_437370_Article.jsp

Crompton, S. (2011). *What's Stressing the Stressed? Main Source of Stress Among Workers*. Statistics Canada. Retrieved July 25, 2015 from http://www.statcangc.ca/pub11-008-x/2011002/article/11562-eng.htm

Goldberg, J. (2014). The Effects of Stress on Your Body. WebMD. Retrieved July 24, 2015 from http://www.webmd.com/balance/stress-management/effects-of-stress-on-your-body

CHAPTER 2

Dyer, W. (2001). *10 Secrets for Success and Inner Peace*. China: Hay House SA.

Goudreau, J. (2013). 12 Ways to Eliminate Stress at Work. *Forbes*. Retrieved July 24, 2015 from http://www.forbes.com/sites/jennagoudreau/2013/03/20/12-ways-to-eliminate-stress-at-work/

Gregoire, G. (2013, August 9). How Changing Breathing Can Change Your Life. *Huffington Post*. Retrieved July 27, 2015 from http://www.huffingtonpost.com/2013/08/09/breathing-health_n_3696302.html

Mertl, S. (2013, May 24). Canada Ranks 3rd Last When it Comes to Paid Vacations. *Daily Brew*. Retrieved December 3, 2015 from https:ca.news.yahoo.com/blogs/dailybrew/Canada-ranks-3rd-last-comes-paid-vacation-days-202727220.html

Robinson, L. et al. (2015). Relaxation Techniques for Stress Relief. HelpGuide.org. Retrieved July 25, 2015 from http://www.helpguide.org/articles/stress/relaxation-techniques-for-stress-relief.htm

Strasser, S. (2015, September 7). America's National Vacation Problem. BBC News. Retrieved September 20, 2015 from http://www.bbc.com/news/world-us-canada-34123906

Thompson, H. (2007). Research Uncovers Causes of Catastrophic Leadership Failures. High Performance Systems Inc. Retrieved July 24, 2015 from http://www.hpsys.com/articles/stress, emotionalintelligenceandleaderperformance.html

Turcotte, M. (2011). Commuting to Work: Results of the 2010 General Social Survey. Statistics Canada. Retrieved July 25, 2015 from http://www.statcan.gc.ca/pub/11-008-x/2011002/article/11531-eng.htm

UFCW Canada. *Health and Safety*. Retrieved July 24, 2015 from http://www.ufcw.ca/index.php?
option=com_content&view=article&id=39&Itemid=77&lang=en

CHAPTER 3

Blitz, J., & Brody, J. (producer). (2010). *Lucky*. United States: Big Beach Films.

CHAPTER 4

Hazelton, D. (1990). *The Courage to See*. Deerfield Beach, FL: Health Communications, Inc.

CHAPTER 6

Division of Sleep Medicine at Harvard Medical School, (2007, December 18). Sleep and Disease Risk.
Healthy Sleep. Retrieved August 11, 2015 from http://healthysleep.med.harvard.edu/health
y/matters/consequences

National Sleep Foundation, (2015, February 2). National Sleep Foundation Recommends New Sleep
Durations. Retrieved January 26, 2016 from http://www.sleepfoundation.org/media-center/
press-release/national-sleep-foundation-recommends-new-sleep-times

Public Health Agency of Canada, (2011, January 20). Benefits of Physical Activity. Retrieved
August 12, 2015 from http://www.phac-aspc.gc.ca/hp-ps/hl-mvs/pa-ap/02paap-eng.php

The Canadian Centre on Substance Abuse, (2014). *Competencies for Canada's Substance Abuse
Workforce*. Ottawa, ON: Canadian Centre on Substance Abuse.

The World Health Organization (2014, August). Mental Health: A State of Well-being. Retrieved
January 24, 2016 from http://www.who.int/features/factfiles/mental_health/en/

CHAPTER 7

Davis, J. (2014). 5 Ways Pets Can Improve Your Health. WebMD. Retrieved August 15, 2015
from http://www.webmd.com/hypertension-high-blood-pressure/features/health-benefits-
of-pets

Emmons, R. (2010, November 16). Why Gratitude is Good. *Greater Good*. Retrieved August 13,
2015 from http://www.greatergood.berkeley.edu/article/item/why_gratitude_is_good

Mahoney, S. (2011, December 2). How Love Keeps You Healthy. Retrieved January 25, 2016 from
http://www.prevention/com/sex.marriage/how-love-keeps-you-healthy

Olsteen, J. (2010). *It's Your Time*. New York, NY: Free Press.

This is the Age of Ubuntu. *A "Touching" Story*. Retrieved from http://www.harisingh.com/
UbuntuAge.htm

Acknowledgements

In no particular order, special thanks to:

Arlene Jorgenson, Donaldo Canales, Jen Falastein, Patrick Falastein, James Siemens, and the Saskatoon Sexual Assault & Information Centre.

About the Author

After persevering through mental health issues and addiction, Allan has learned valuable life lessons that have guided him on an incredible path of success. Today, he is a sought-after keynote speaker who has gained national attention for his engaging style and captivating approach.

Allan is a best-selling author of four books, three of which have been incorporated into college curricula. His writing has been published in countless national magazines, and Allan has been featured on several television and radio programs.

Allan has spent years working as an addiction counsellor, clinical case manager, and instructor at several colleges. He lives in Saskatoon with his beautiful wife, four boys, four dogs, and a tank of fish.

For more information or to inquire about booking Allan for a presentation, please visit: **www.allankehler.com**